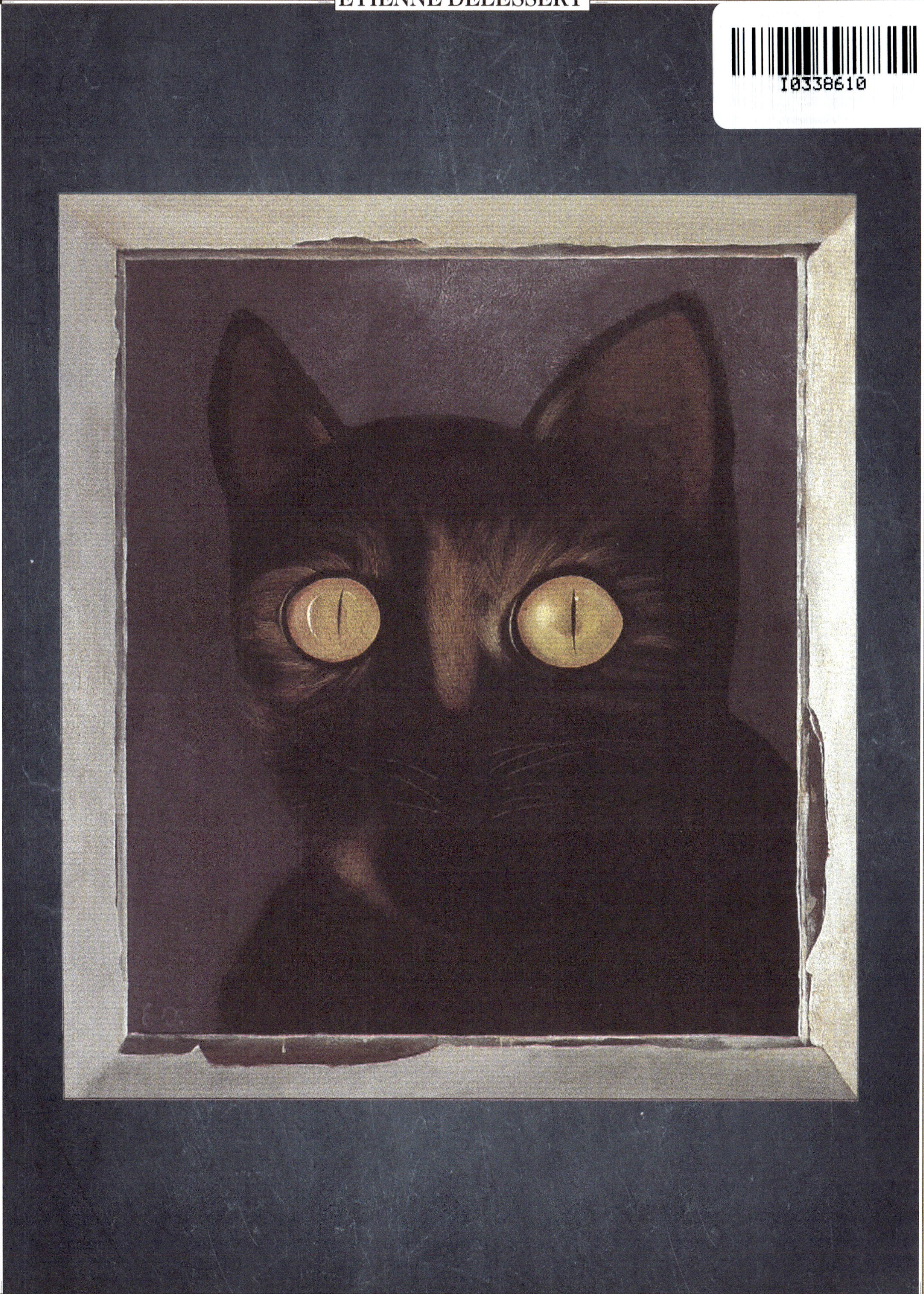

PUBLISHER'S LETTER
BY MICHAEL GERBER

STARDUST MEMORIES

If you're anything like me, every October 9th you think of that guy over there -->

I gotta be honest—the world hasn't made one goddamn bit of sense to me since John Lennon got shot. Who's up for a re-do?

In December 1980 I was 11. I much prefer being 50; I have a job, I have sex, and can watch any movie I want. Turning back the clock would be a lousy deal for me, personally, but I'm totally willing to do it, for everyone else's sake.

For example: we had a president whose biggest flaw was that people thought he was too nice. Think of waking up to that everyday. It was goddamn heaven. You could *relax*.

Plus—though they won't admit it now—folks were having sex constantly, and the only way it could kill you is if their spouse was an excellent shot. There's something old-fashioned and nice about that. Then along came an STD that killed all the artists, but left all the investment bankers. *Oof.*

Music was better in 1980, because you could make a living from it. Ditto books and magazines. Every new business wasn't about addiction or a desire to avoid human contact. If you wanted to look at porn, you had to work at it; this gave masturbation a real sense of accomplishment. (Remember, I was 11.)

Of course, the economy wasn't great. People were worried about inflation. But you know who inflation hurts? The 1%. You know who it's great for? People who have student loans or credit card debt. "Here, Chase, take this $50,000 bill and get outta my face." Tell me that doesn't sound freaking awesome.

MICHAEL GERBER (@mgerber937) is Editor & Publisher of *The American Bystander*.

Did we worry about nuclear war? Sure. But the only reason we're not worrying about it now is there's this new way to die that's somehow even worse. It's like Humanity got together and said, "Sure, killing every lifeform on the planet is bad, but can we do it more slowly? How can we really *savor* it?" Global warming combines the helpless terror of nuclear war with the agony of starving to death. Good job everybody!

Also, in 1980, nobody had the sneaking suspicion that the leaders of the US and USSR were kinda rooting for Armageddon. I think Vlad wants the permafrost to melt, so Russia can get a bunch of new farmland and have five years of *really sticking it to everybody* before the unfrozen bubonic plague hits. And can you imagine Jimmy Carter openly resenting the possibility that the world might go on without him? The guy who got on TV and said, "Please put on a sweater so we burn less fossil fuel. Trust me, it'll be better for everyone."

1980 was sensible, and I say this with full knowledge of the fashion and hair. Today? Not sensible. Today, some of us would rather *drown* than pay more taxes. Some of us today ignore everything but some poorly ret-conned fan-fic cooked up 2000 years ago by Yahweh-knows-who. Of all the people to listen to, why them? Why not, say, Albert Einstein? Einstein didn't give a damn what people did in bed, what anyone ate, or whether you mixed linen and wool. Because Einstein had a *life*. Einstein wasn't *crazy*.

Look, I'm not saying that 1980 was perfect. The Rubik's Cube for example: I could never get more than one side. But back in the day, when a fellow American got done dirty by some bigshot, the rest of us tried to make it right because—alien concept—someday we might be the ones needing help. Bad apples were expected to go to jail, not gather a group of gibbering knuckleheads around themselves and make a run for the presidency. *Then win!*

So we didn't have little computers in our pocket, so what. Go read Twitter—most of us can't *handle* little computers in our pocket. In 1980, Woody Allen seemed like just a comedian; Bill Cosby too. Yes, people smoked cigarettes in airplanes, and New York was still sticky to the touch, but then again, the Beatles might get back together. John Belushi was still alive. Tell me *that* doesn't sound great.

In 1980, a beard still meant something. We didn't ignore scientists for fun. Charging $7.50 for a tiny little cupcake was not a workable business model. If some rich dork announced that he was going to dig a members-only subway from New York to San Francisco, or started his own private NASA, people would say, "That guy needs to pay more taxes"—and it would *happen*. But it wouldn't come to that, because in 1980, he would be getting laid. *Frequently.*

In 1980, you could see a movie with Nazis in it without worrying about who the guy sitting next to you was rooting for. It was a nice feeling, young people, it really was.

Things that didn't exist in 1980: bottled water, antibiotic-resistant diseases, SUVs, revenge porn, Facebook.

I could go on all day, we both know I could, and we both know I want to. But I'm going to stop, because time travel won't invent itself. We all have to quit complaining, and get on the stick.

Set the dial to December 7, 1980—who's with me? And who wants to go tell John and Yoko to maybe catch a late movie? *Stardust Memories* is at the Ziegfeld. It's not one of Woody's best, but trust me you two—it's better than the alternative. B

STEPHEN KRONINGER

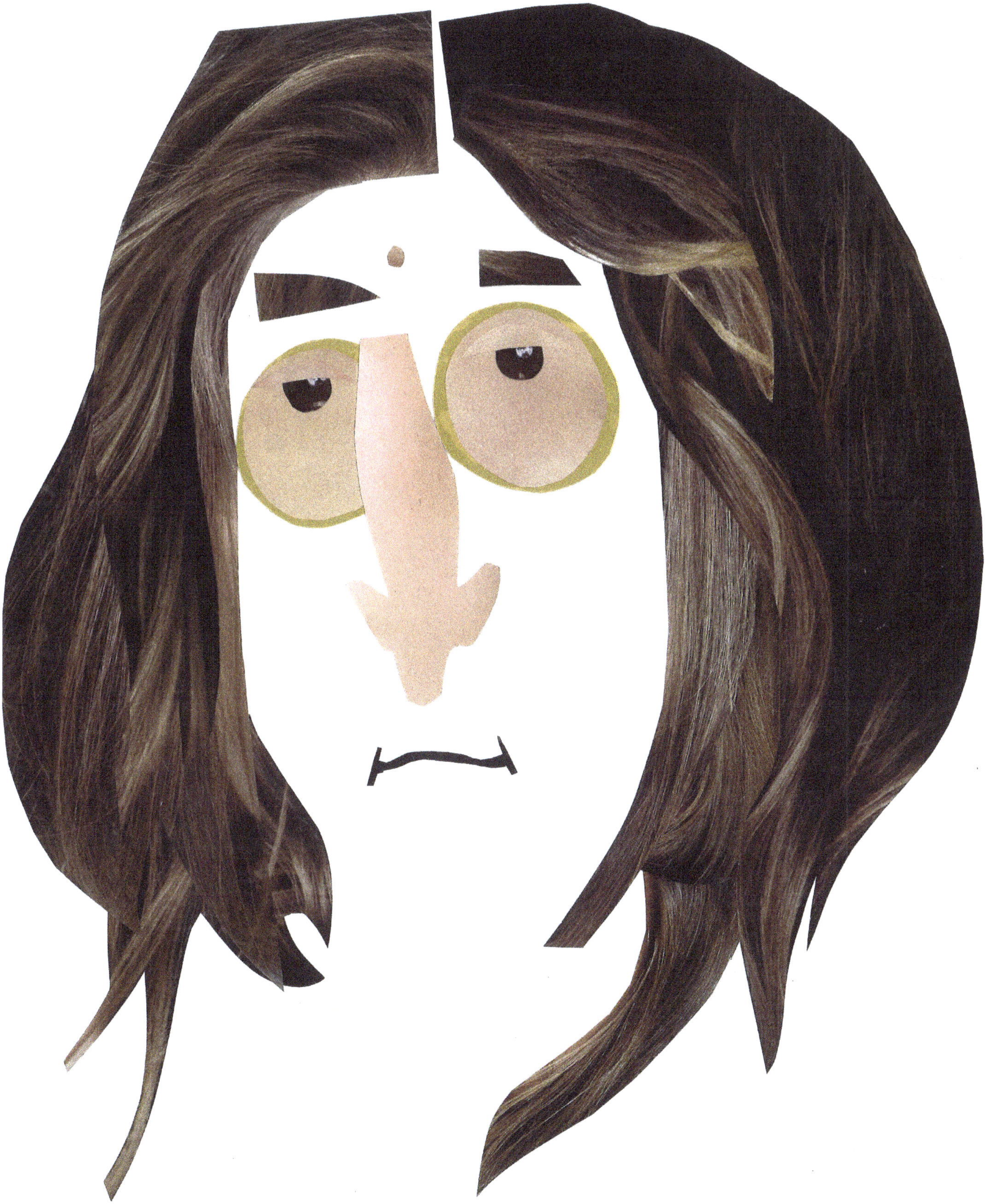

TABLE OF CONTENTS

The AMERICAN BYSTANDER
#13 • Vol. 4, No. 1 • Halloween 2019

ZOE MATTHIESSEN

EDITOR & PUBLISHER
Michael Gerber
HEAD WRITER
Brian McConnachie
SENIOR EDITOR
Alan Goldberg

ORACLE Steve Young
STAFF LIAR P.S. Mueller
INTREPID TRAVELER
Mike Reiss
AGENTS OF THE SECOND BYSTANDER INTERNATIONAL
Joey Green, Craig Boreth, Matt Kowalick, Neil Mitchell, Maxwell Ziegler
MANAGING EDITOR EMERITA
Jennifer Boylan

CONTRIBUTORS
Lucas Adams, Penny Barr, Charley Barsotti, Lou Beach, George Booth, Valerie Breiman, Dylan Brody, Justin Courter, Howard Cruse, Joe Dator, Etienne Delessert, Chris Dingman, Ben Doyle, Larry Doyle, Marques Duggans, Ivan Ehlers, Meg Favreau, Emily Flake, Rick Geary, Sam Gross, Lance Hansen, Ron Hauge, Brandon Hicks, Tim Hunt, Ted Jouflas, Paul Karasik, Farley Katz, Lars Kenseth, Jennifer Kim, Stephen Kroninger, Peter Kuper, Rob Kutner, Mary Lawton, Stan Mack, Glenn Marshall, Scott Marshall, Zoe Matthiessen, Rick Meyerowitz, Risa Mickenberg, Lydia Oxenham, Matt Percival, Michael Pershan, K.A. Polzin, Karen Rile, Laurie Rosenwald, E.L. Savage, Alex Schmidt, Cris Shapan, Jim Siergey, Richard Seltzer, Mick Stevens, Lexi Stevenson, Ed Subitzky, Aaron Thier, D. Watson, Steve Young, and Sheryl Zohn.

THANKS TO
Kate Powers, Lanky Bareikis, Jon Schwarz, Alleen Schultz, Molly Bernstein, Joe Lopez, Eliot Ivanhoe, Neil Gumenick, Kate Ingold, Greg & Patricia Gerber and many others.

NAMEPLATES BY
Mark Simonson
ISSUE CREATED BY
Michael Gerber

Vol. 4, No. 1. ©2019 Good Cheer LLC, all rights reserved. Proudly produced in California, USA. **A.M.V.G.**

DEPARTMENTS
Frontispiece: "Black Cat" **by Etienne Delessert** 1
Publisher's Letter **by Michael Gerber** 2
A Contest! 7
The Good Stuff: Art, Part 2 8
News and Notes 10
The Caboose: "Hurricane Watch" **by D. Watson** 76

GALLIMAUFRY
Risa Mickenberg, Ivan Ehlers, Chris Dingman, Lars Kenseth, Karen Rile, Penny Barr, Rob Kutner, Jennifer Finney Boylan, Mary Lawton, E.L. Savage, Lydia Oxenham, Joe Dator, Sheryl Zohn, Farley Katz, K.A. Polzin, Jim Siergey, Michael Pershan, Stan Mack, Richard Seltzer.

SHORT STUFF
Hair Cut Blues **by Rick Geary** 5
Barely Credible **by Justin Courter** 23
City Life **by Jennifer Kim** 24
Blue Mastodon **by Lou Beach** 26
Actually, My Toddler is Playing 4-D Chess
  by Alex Schmidt 28
Five Basic Life-Lessons That *Clueless* Totally Nailed!
  by Meg Favreau 30

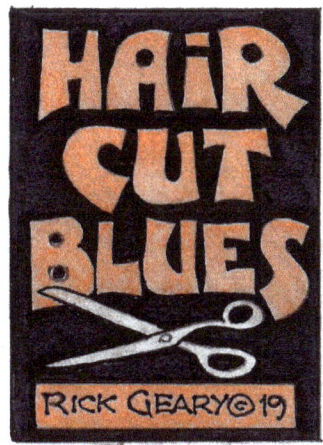

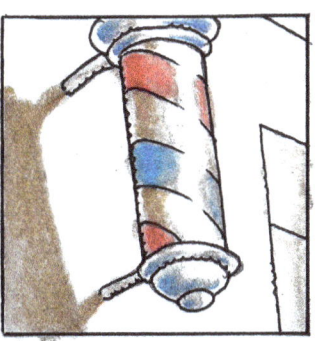

HAIR CUT BLUES
RICK GEARY © 19
AS A KID, NOTHING EQUALED THE TORTURE AND EMBARRASSMENT OF A HAIR CUT.
MY MOTHER PERSONALLY ESCORTED ME TO THE LOCAL BARBER.
AND GAVE HIM VERY SPECIFIC DIRECTIONS: "PART IT ON THE LEFT..."
"AND DON'T GIVE HIM THAT SHAVED OR PEELED LOOK ON THE SIDES."
VITALIS
AND WHAT'S LEFT SLICK BACK WITH VITALIS.
THIS CONTINUED FARTHER INTO MY TEENS THAN I'D LIKE TO ADMIT.
YOU SEE, MOM GREW UP IN A RURAL TOWN WITH A VERY RIGID SOCIAL STRUCTURE.
AS A "TOWN GIRL," SHE LOOKED WITH DISTAIN UPON THE FARM KIDS...
BOYS WITH AN UNKEMPT MOP, OR AN UNAPPEALING BOWL-AND-SCISSORS CUT.
END THE WAR
LSD NOT LBJ
SMASH THE STATE
THEN THE 60'S ARRIVED AND THE EVIL HAIR CUT REGIME WAS VANQUISHED.
CLOSED
THE OLD BARBER-SHOPS CLOSED THEIR DOORS.
THE AGE OF DISORDER HAD ARRIVED!
I ENTERED FULL REBELLION ...
AND HAVE REMAINED THERE...
TO THIS DAY!

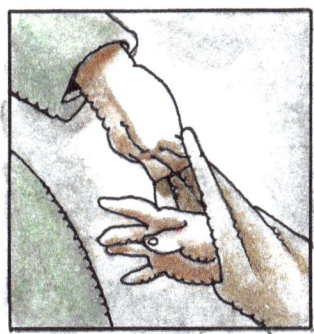

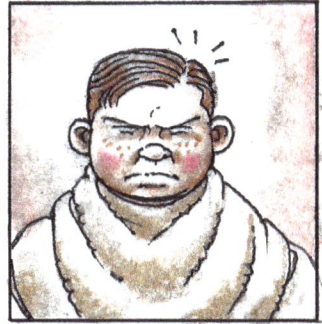

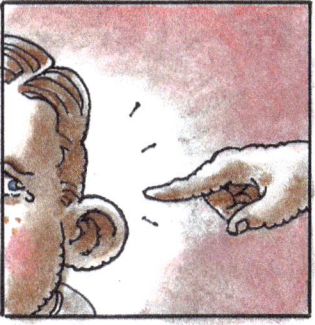

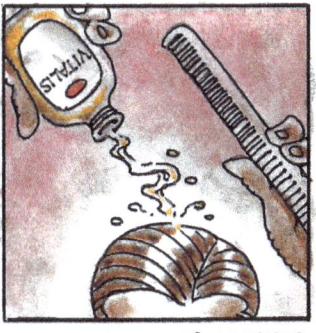

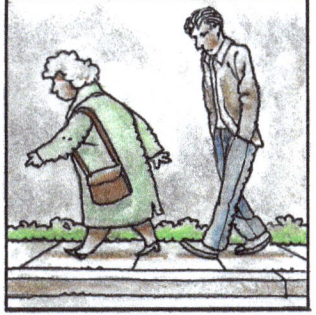

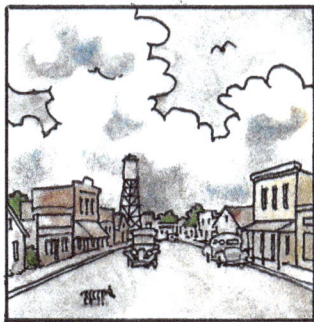

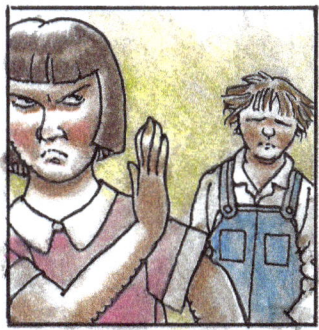

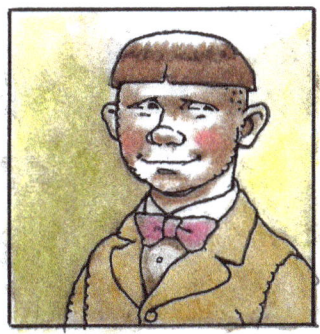

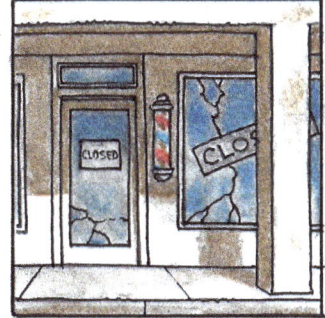

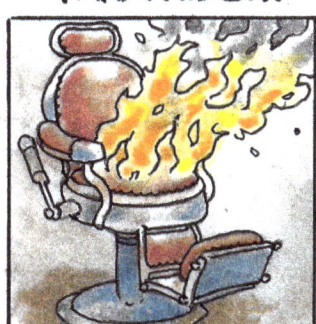

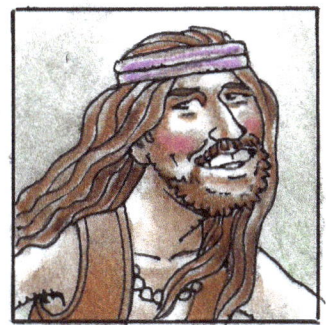

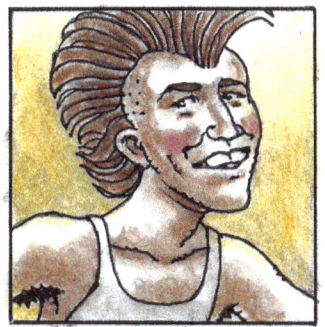

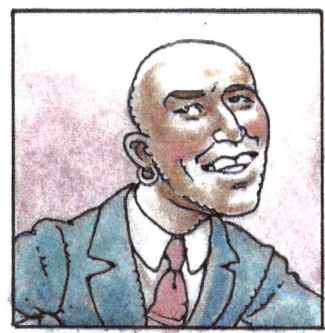

FEATURES

Tele-Ween *by Steve Young* 33
In the Skyscraper! *by Ed Subitzky* 34
Amazon Prime Suspect
  by Laurie Rosenwald & Risa Mickenberg 36
Final Instructions *by Larry & Ben Doyle* 37
Trump Illustration *by Rick Meyerowitz* 38
Back Issues *by Cris Shapan* 41
I Saw Milton Berle's Schlong *by Valerie Breiman* 45
Snacks of the Future *by Lucas Adams* 49
Preparations for Flu Season *by Aaron Thier* 51
I Was a Jewish Druid *by Dylan Brody* 57
Z*ggy Tuesdays *by Paul Karasik* 60
Very Disappointed in Ozzy *by Ted Jouflas* 62
Some Words From the Guys In Charge *by Howard Cruse* ... 66
Cartoons *by Lexi Stevenson* 68

OUR BACK PAGES

Letter From Melania *by Emily Flake* 71
What Am I Doing Here?: Patagonia *by Mike Reiss* 73
P.S. Mueller Thinks Like This *by P.S. Mueller* 75

CARTOONS & ILLUSTRATIONS BY

Etienne Delessert, Scott Marshall, Stephen Kroninger, Zoe Matthiessen, George Booth, Sam Gross, Jim Siergey, Glenn Marshall, Lou Beach, Lance Hansen, Marques Duggans, Charley Barsotti, Stan Mack, Mick Stevens, Matt Percival, Brandon Hicks, Peter Kuper, Emily Flake, Tim Hunt, P.S. Mueller.

.... ◆ ....

Sam's Spot

COVER

Some of our covers are so good they could conjure an entire book, and when **ARMANDO VEVE** delivered his art, a whole story blossomed in my brain. This wired witch is speeding to her digs downtown, a well-appointed brownstone on West 11th between Bleecker and West 4th. She received the deed some years ago from a grateful Secretary of State Seward, in exchange for "Mr. Stonewall Jackson's unfortunate accident." More recently she's occupied herself by magically manipulating the stock market; she delights in dropping enormous, anonymous college scholarships into the laps of earnest high school Wiccans. Most afternoons she can be found at Tartine, eating pastries and slipping love potions into unsuspecting patrons' teacups. She agrees that the neighborhood isn't what it used to be but—being 227—knows it never was.

ACKNOWLEDGMENTS

All material is ©2019 its creators, all rights reserved; please do not reproduce or distribute it without written consent of the creators and *The American Bystander*. All material is new.

THE AMERICAN BYSTANDER, Vol. 4, No. 1, (978-0-578-60202-8). Publishes ~4x/year. ©2019 by Good Cheer LLC. No part of this magazine can be reproduced, in whole or in part, by any means, without the written permission of the Publisher. For this and other queries, email *Publisher@americanbystander.org*, or write: Michael Gerber, Publisher, *The American Bystander*, 1122 Sixth St., #403, Santa Monica, CA 90403. **Subscribe at www.patreon.com/bystander.** Other info can be found at www.americanbystander.org.

A CONTEST!

Who Carved These?

One of our excellent contributors sent me snapshots of their jack-o'lanterns. Who is the artist? Send your guess to ***publisher@americanbystander.org***. The first correct answer will receive a Mystery Book from Mike's library.

MEG FAVREAU

THE EYE *recommends* **OWNING A BLANKET**. *You can* **SIT ON TOP** *of it,* **HIDE UNDER** *it, or* **BURRITO ROLL** *in it. It is a* **STATUS SYMBOL** *that shows you* **ENJOY COMFORT**…*If you are* **THINKING** *about* **CURLING UP IN A HOLE** *for the* **NEXT TWENTY YEARS**, *make sure you* **ASK** *whether the* **HOLE** *is* **RENT-CONTROLLED**…**WISH** *you made* **DIFFERENT CHOICES**? *Just* **REMOVE** *an "R" to turn your* **REGRETS** *into* **EGRETS**…*When you are* **SAD**, *it can be* **EASY TO FORGET** *that there are* **OTHER EMOTIONS**. *But there are! If there weren't,* **SADNESS** *wouldn't be* **CALLED "SADNESS,"** *it would simply be called* **"THE EMOTION."** *(Twitter: @THE_EYE_FRIEND.)*

READER SERVICE
THE GOOD STUFF: ART, PART 2
No, that hack in Lascaux didn't make it

Last issue, we ran the first half of our contributors' answers to the following question: "Which art/illustration/cartooning books are must-own? Which helped make you the person you are today?" Thankfully, they took that last question in a spirit of celebration, not of blaming.

Miracle Man by Alan Moore (*Shannon Wheeler*)
Monster Rally by Charles Addams (*Ken Krimstein*)
More Drawings by Heinrich Kley (*Rich Sparks*)
My Favorite Thing is Monsters by Emil Ferris (*Jim Siergey, James Finn Garner*)
The Naked Cartoonist by Bob Mankoff (*Matt Percival*)
Never Eat Anything Bigger Than Your Head by B. Kliban (*Ron Hauge, Andrew Weldon*)
The New Yorker Album: 1925–1950 (*Sport Murphy, John Jonik*)
No Comment by Nurit Karlin (*Ken Krimstein*)
Nuts by Gahan Wilson (*Shannon Wheeler, Larry Doyle*)
Oh Happy Happy by Chuck Saxon (*Mort Gerberg*)
One Hundred Demons by Lynda Barry (*Andrew Weldon*)
The Pain—When Will It End? By Tim Krieder (*Andrew Weldon*)
PASSIONELLA by Jules Feiffer (*Sam Henderson*)
Peanuts by Charles M. Schultz (*Larry Doyle*)
The Penguin Leunig by Michael Leunig (*Andrew Weldon*)
The Perry Bible Fellowship by Nicholas Gurewitch (*Andrew Weldon*)
Persepolis by Marjane Satrapi (*Melissa Balmain*)
Peter Arno's Cartoon Revue by Peter Arno (*Ron Hauge*)
Peter Saul: A Retrospective ed. by Robert Storr (*Lance Hansen*)
Philip Guston: Nixon Drawings: 1971 & 1975 (*Lance Hansen*)
Prairie State Blues; comic strips & graphic tales by Bill Bergeron (*David Chelsea*)
Private Eye—A Cartoon History, ed. by Nick Newman (*Matt Percival*)
RanXerox by Tamburini and Liberatore (*Nick Spooner*)
Revealing Illustrations: The Art of James McMullan (*David Chelsea*)
The Ridiculously Expensive MAD (*Sam Henderson*)
R. Crumb's Head Comix (*David Chelsea*)
Ronald Searle's America, edited by Matt Jones (*Steve Jones*)
Rube Goldberg Vs The Machine Age (*Sport Murphy*)
Rudy in Hollywood by William Overgard (*Larry Doyle*)
Saul Steinberg by Deirdre Bair (*Matt Percival*)
The Secret History of Wonder Woman by Jill Lepore (*Patrick Kennedy*)
Sick, Sick, Sick by Jules Feiffer (*Larry Doyle*)
Sigmund Freud by Ralph Steadman (*Joe Ciardiello, Rich Sparks*)
Sin City by Frank Miller (*Shannon Wheeler*)
The Smithsonian Collection of Comic Books (*Sam Henderson*)
The Smithsonian Collection of Newspaper Comics (*Sam Henderson, Adam Koford*)
Snake 'n' Bacon's Cartoon Caberet by Michael Kupperman (*Andrew Weldon*)

Speak Up You Tiny Fool! by John Glashan (*Ben Katchor*)
Steinberg Le Masque by Michel Butor and Harold Rosenberg (*Matt Percival, John Jonik*)
Stranger Than Life by M.K. Brown (*David Chelsea*)
Superpen by Edward Sorel (*Ron Hauge*)
Tantrum by Jules Feiffer (*Larry Doyle*)
The Tattooed Sailor by Andre Francois (*John Jonik*)
Think Good Thoughts About a Pussycat by George Booth (*Ron Hauge*)
The Ten-Cent Plague by David Hajdu (*Lance Hansen*)
Theories of Everything by Roz Chast (*Andrew Weldon*)
This Is Everything I Know by Spike Trotman (*Geoffrey Golden*)
Thomas Nast, His Period and His Pictures by Albert Paine (*Ron Hauge*)
A Thurber Carnival by James Thurber (*John Jonik*)
Tiny Footprints by B. Kliban (*Nick Spooner, Ian Baker, Ken Krimstein*)
Trots & Bonnie Collection, if there was one by Shary Flenniken (*Shannon Wheeler, Larry Doyle*)
Trump Magazine: The Complete Collection by Harvey Kurtzman, et al. (*Lance Hansen, Will Pfeifer*)
National Lampoon's **Truly Tasteless Cartoons** (*Ian Baker, Andrew Weldon*)
Two Guys Fooling Around With The Moon by B. Kliban (*Nick Spooner, Ian Baker, Ken Krimstein*)
Understanding Comics by Scott McCloud (*Geoffrey Golden, K.A. Polzin, David Ostow*)
Understanding Kafka, by David Zane Mairowitz and Robert Crumb (*Jeff Kulik*)
Upfront by Bill Mauldin (*Jim Siergey*)
Vision In Motion: Laszlo Moholy-Nagy (*Sport Murphy*)
Watchmen by Alan Moore (*Shannon Wheeler*)
Whack Your Porcupine by B. Kliban (*Nick Spooner*)
WHAT AM I DOING HERE? by Abner Dean (*Sam Henderson*)
Why I Hate Saturn by Kyle Baker (*Larry Doyle*)
Will Eisner: Comics and Sequential Art (*Joe Oesterle*)
Will Elder: The Mad Playboy of Art (*Will Pfeifer*)
The World Encyclopedia of Comics by Maurice Horn (*Ron Hauge*)
The World of Chas Addams by Charles Addams (*Ron Hauge*)
The World of George Price by George Price (*Leonard Stokes*)
The World of John Glashan by John Glashan (*Ben Katchor*)
The Worst Thing I've Ever Done by Ted Rall (*Andrew Weldon*)
Writings & Drawings—Mervyn Peake (*Rich Sparks*)
You Are Here by Kyle Baker (*Larry Doyle*)
Your Mother is a Remarkable Woman by Sam Gross (*ian Baker*)
Zany Afternoons by Bruce McCall (*Ron Hauge, Andrew Weldon*)
Zippy the Pinhead 'Annuals' by Bill Griffith (*K.A. Polzin*) **B**

NEWS & NOTES

I cannot believe I have to say this: Contributors are not allowed to die without permission. (That goes for readers, too.)

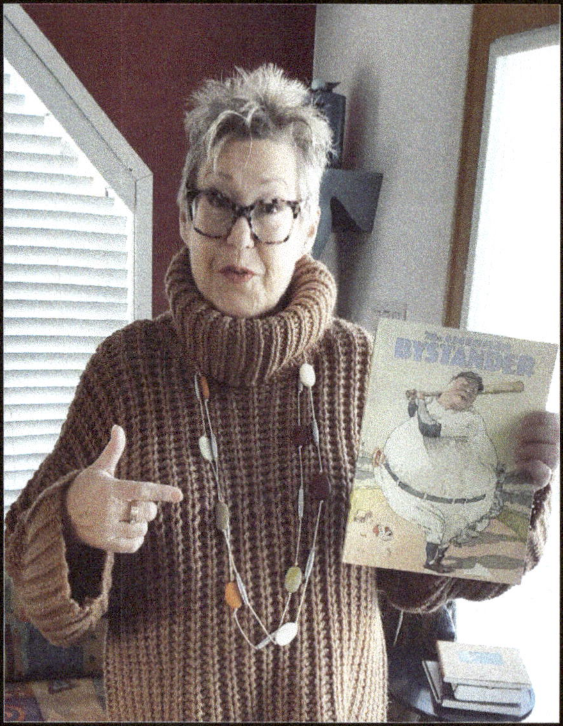
BYSTANDER

A FRIEND TO THE END: *This photo was, I'm told, on Penny's memorial board. What a compliment.*

Penny Barr's email of September 4th started as usual: "Hey Chief!" That always made me feel good, you know, like an old-time magazine editor—Ben Hecht, *The Front Page,* Hildy Johnson, "get me rewrite." Instead of some overeducated, undermedicated, crumb-covered kook sitting in his boxers in a corner of the living room, peering one-eyed at InDesign through a miasma of B.O. and broken dreams.

I'd told Penny the brutal truth, but her kindness was too big for that. "Hey Chief! Hope you're well. I," she lied, "am doing fine."

In fact, she was dealing with a recurrence of stage four cancer. But Penny would never tell me that, because she was preparing to pitch. Penny knew that I'd run anything if she played "the wounded bird," as Lenny Bruce called it; but she didn't play like that. She was, after all, Canadian.

"Pen, I like it, but it feels like Instagram." I rejected the cartoon, softening the blow by reminding her that she had her regular spot in this issue (*see page 14*), and that I looked forward to seeing whatever she came up with next.

There was no next. A few weeks later, I got an email from a person I didn't know, 2019's version of a phone call from your mother at 3 A.M. A very nice lady named Christine told me that, the night before, Penny had died. "Penny loved *Bystander,*" Christine said after I'd called. "She loved reading it, and loved contributing to it. She talked about it regularly."

Well, I never knew any of *that*; there simply hadn't been time. A full 50% of our chats had consisted of me complimenting Penny on the clearly gratuitous but undeniably cheerful nudity she always managed to sneak into her cartoons. The other 50% was a mutual gnashing of teeth over Canada Post, which sees "American" on our cover and goes into some sort of non-delivering passive-aggressive fugue state. God knows we Yanks deserve it, especially now, but readers have their limits, even Canadians.

In the course of playing our mournful games of Carmen Sandiego we'd talked about my visiting Toronto, and maybe even launching a *Canadian Bystander,* as a sort of flanking maneuver.

But now that won't happen, at least not with Penny as my tour guide, introducing me to all her pals from the *Globe and Mail*, or her rock band. I'll never get to see Pen's floating home (featured in *Bystander* #12), nor compliment her one last time on all those cartoon bosoms, so friendly the nipples look like they're smiling.

I adored Penny Barr's talent, and she fit in perfectly here at *The American Bystander.* Because she loved the magazine, I know she is with us still, and will be sure to invoke her help and her blessing whenever we mail issues. "O Penny of Toronto, protect us! O Patroness of all Canadian Bystanders and our foreign subscribers scattered about the world, please pray for us your children and protect our mailout, during this the time of our need. Make sure all our issues get to readers safely, unmangled and unbent, with poly bags unopened and covers still securely attached; unmolested by censors, nor stolen by roommates, nor gnawed by raccoons; nor defaced by those of little brain, nor indeed by parents, offended by thine ever-cheerful knockers, nor teachers sadly deficient in humor. O Penny, protect us thou from lawyers, and those possessing peculiar and alarming political opinions, in every way keeping these, thine issues, safe from harm, repelling naughty people of every description, wherever they might be. We ask this in your name, amen."

Goodbye, Penny. And take *that*, Canada Post. B

COMING APRIL 2020 FROM FANTAGRAPHICS BOOKS

The art of B.K. Taylor, ripped from the pages of *National Lampoon*:

I Think He's Crazy!

BY B.K. Taylor

Including a forward by Tim Allen (*Home Improvement*) and backword by R.L. Stine (*Goosebumps*).

Exclusive offer for *American Bystander* readers: Order this book from the Fantagraphics website and use the promo code BYSTANDER to get 20% off!

FANTAGRAPHICS.COM/BK-TAYLOR

A graphic novel by famed artist
Robert Grossman

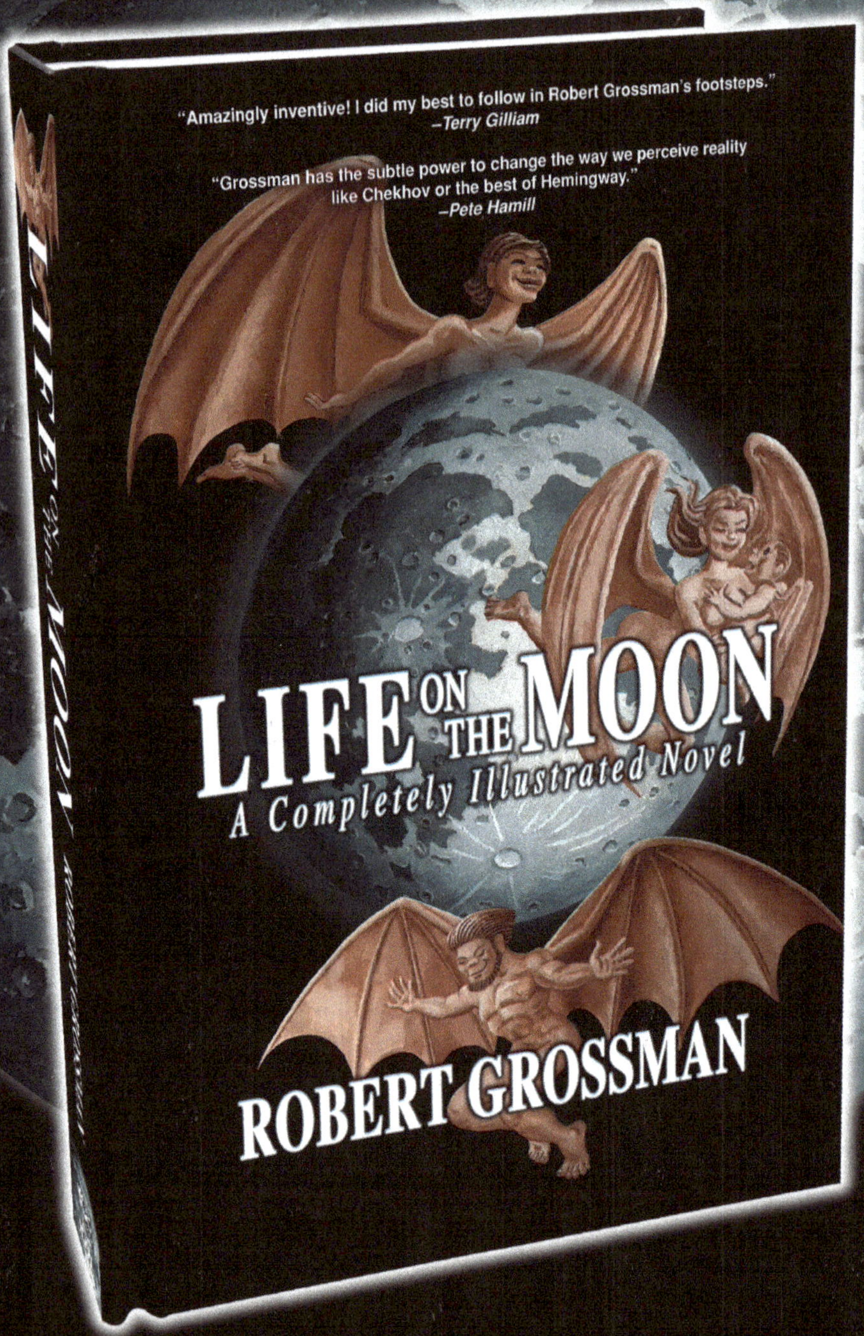

LIFE ON THE MOON
A Completely Illustrated Novel
ROBERT GROSSMAN

"History and fantasy join forces!"
—Rolling Stone

"Amazingly inventive! I did my best to follow in Robert Grossman's footsteps."
—Terry Gilliam

"Like Chekhov or the best of Hemingway."
—Pete Hamill

YoeBooks.com

Gallimaufry

"Look on my Works, ye bitches and despair!"

CAUTIONARY TALES.

Permanent Spinal Damage

Diane Lockhart was sitting in the driver's seat in her boyfriend's car and she was wearing her Dr. Scholl's and she hit the gas by accident and the shoe got caught on the gas pedal and she drove the car into the back of the Pathmark and got permanent spinal damage.

Keith Herrara's Pierced Eardrum

In archery, Keith Herrara was messing around with these arrows and he put them in his ears so it looked like he got shot in the head? And then he did a jumping jack and his arm hit one of the arrows and it went right into his ear and it pierced his eardrum and he was deaf in that ear from then on.

How We Both Got Burnt Bangs

No so one time Kris Korchikas and I were smoking a bowl and she went to light it with a lighter and the lighter was turned all the way up, and it totally singed her bangs and her eyebrows. And we were just like, oh my god, dying laughing, and then she passed me the bowl and the lighter and I totally forgot and my bangs were like, just crisped, and we were just like oh… my… god and then we had to go back inside with both of our bangs burnt and everyone was just like what happened to you two?

Why You Have To Pay Attention When You Use The Paper Cutter

Mrs. Files was talking to someone and she wasn't paying attention while she was using the paper cutter and she sliced the very top of her pointer finger all the way through except for a little bit of skin that was holding it on. Her whole fingertip was hanging there just from a piece of skin.

—Risa Mickenberg

SOME TIPS.

Looking for a new cell phone but confused by all the options? Relax—we here at *American Mafioso* have you covered. Here are 10 simple tips:.

1. Don't be an idiot.
2. Don't be a fucking idiot.
3. What are you, some kind of fucking idiot?
4. You like the phone? So fucking buy it already.
5. Pink. You want a pink phone. Fine, get the fucking pink phone.
6. Where's the john?
7. What kinda store doesn't have a john?
8. Swear to God, I'm gonna piss on the carpet.
9. A good rule of thumb when shopping for cell phones is: shop in a store that has a fucking john!
10. Do me a favor. Next time, go shopping by yourself.

—Chris Dingman

TANNER OZYMANDIAS.

I met a traveler from an antiquing land, known as Connecticut,

Who said—"Two vast and neckless WASPs from Darien

Stand at a country club fundraiser… near them, in the sand trap,

Half-drunk their spoiled brat lies about reading Tolstoy,

Whose frown, and wrinkled lip, and sneer of cold command,

Tell that its sculptor really should have pulled back on the botox

I mean, he's like what, thirty? It just looks odd.

And on the auction pedestal, a dinner with Ira Glass.

And this kid bids five-hundred thousand dollars. He does not have five-hundred thousand dollars. And he said, 'My name is Tanner Ozymandias, do you know who my father is?

Look on my Works, ye bitches and despair!'

Then he just started kind of kicking over folding chairs.

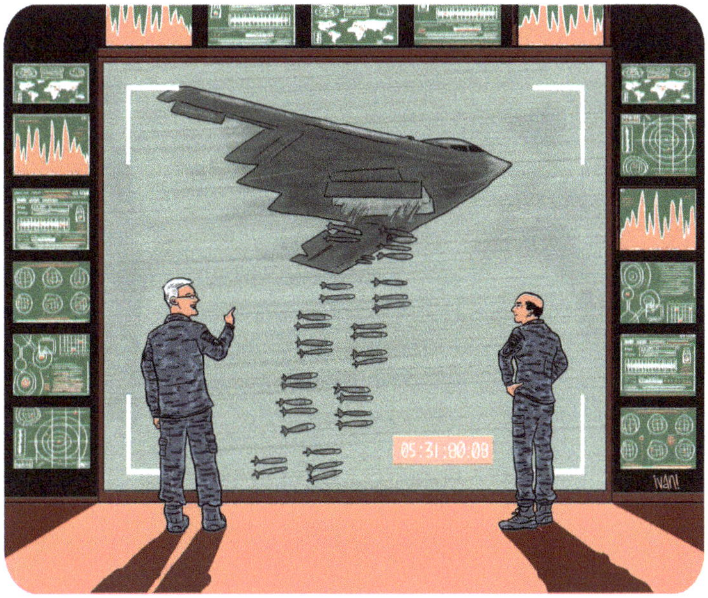
05:31:80:08
ivan!

"Tell me that ain't worth 62 cents of every American dollar."

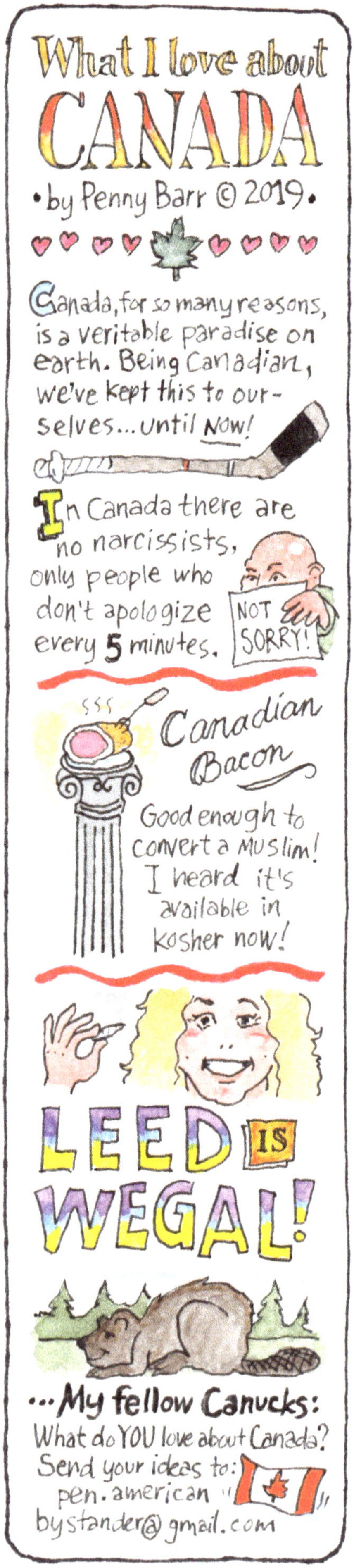
What I love about
CANADA
• by Penny Barr © 2019 •
Canada, for so many reasons, is a veritable paradise on earth. Being Canadian, we've kept this to ourselves...until NOW!
In Canada there are no narcissists, only people who don't apologize every 5 minutes.
NOT SORRY!
Canadian Bacon
Good enough to convert a Muslim! I heard it's available in kosher now!
LEED IS WEGAL!
...My fellow Canucks:
What do YOU love about Canada?
Send your ideas to: pen.american bystander@gmail.com

It was funny, but also a little sad.
Nothing beside remains. Round the disarray
Of that colossal Douche. Security dragged him off.
Across the lone and level ninth green.
The kicked-over folding chairs stretch far away."

—Lars Kenseth

A QUICK START GUIDE.

Congratulations on purchasing CROWN OF SQUIRRELS the versatile new accessory everybody's chittering about! CROWN OF SQUIRRELS is perfect for autumn tabletop centerpieces, trick-or-treating, and Oktoberfest squirrel selfies. Check out the tree pose and more on our award-winning Squirrel Yoga YouTube channel!

Follow these simple instructions to get up and running with your new crown in no time!

Safety first! (Not for use by children under 12.)

Before attempting unbox your CROWN OF SQUIRRELS, prepare yourself by removing any loose-fitting or flowing clothing. Securely tie back or cover long hair, including facial hair.

It is recommended not to consume tree nuts, legumes including peanuts, and seed products for 24 hours prior to unboxing your CROWN OF SQUIRRELS. Before attempting to open the carton, floss teeth and swallow 1-4 ounces antiseptic mouthwash (example: Listerine.)

Always wear gloves when handling the Crown. CROWN OF SQUIRRELS is certified rabies-free, but, as always, when wearing live rodents on your head, a little caution goes a long way.

Now that you've read about Safety, you know everything you need to open your CROWN OF SQUIRRELS, and that's pretty cool! Thank you for your patience. It's time to get squirelly!

Enclose yourself with the unopened carton in an empty, well-ventilated room. Place durable, heavy-duty woven poly screen across HVAC registers. Secure all doors and windows and check that the area is free from cats, dogs, small children, elderly relatives, upholstered furniture, and electronics. You may hear sounds such as skittering, whistling, and/or screaming inside your carton. Do not panic! This is normal.

Spread a 10x12 tarp across the floor and place carton in the center. Your CROWN OF SQUIRRELS carton is packed with genuine (not styrofoam or cornstarch) peanuts. If you don't have a heavy-duty 10x12 tarp, no worries. You can always use a shop vac later.

Make sure the box is right side up! Pull open the tabs *(Fig. 1)* with a smooth and confident gesture. It's important to remain calm as the squirrels are released from the box. Upon release, it is not unusual for the squirrels to swarm throughout the room and climb up your limbs. (See safety instructions, above, concerning loose garments.) If a squirrel or squirrels still manages to scurry up your pant leg, shake legs vigorously and remove pants before proceeding.

Lift crown from carton, brush away any remaining peanut shells, and check to ensure all straps, buckles, and adjustments are secure before each use. Open peanut butter jar (starter sample included) and quickly dab 1 tsp on each crown tip. At this point, your CROWN OF SQUIRRELS should be fully operational.

Place crown on head. Grab your iPhone. Now you're ready for some fun.

—Karen Rile

MINDFULNESS EXERCISES (IN BETA).

You are lying on a warm, sandy beach, the gentle sun kissing your skin, the tang of salt dancing in the air, the sound of a small child calling for his Mommy, affectionately…then more energetically…now in sudden, sharp shrieks, cut off by sounds of struggle and gurgling waters, *Jesus Christ does no one else hear this kid, what is wrong with the parents, why did they even bother to have this child, was it to patch up some other failing piece of their relationship just like is happening to you right now and is all your fault?*

You are sitting in a beautiful, lush garden brimming with endless fertile possibilities, unlike the ones you missed in your 20s-40s—let's review all of those now, shall we?

You are floating on a cloud, a soft, fluffy cloud, just drifting along and waitaminute—clouds are made of ice and dust and NOT SUPPOSED TO BE FLUFFY AND WHY ARE YOUR WRISTS, ANKLES, AND GENITALS RESTRAINED?

You're in your Happy Place, you're in your Happy Place, you're in your Happy Place...

You're flying a kite on a perfect bluesky day, when a beautiful dove floats by, lightly brushing the soft string of the kite, just delicately tipping it into an electrical line, sending a stream of voltage directly into both of your arms. You awaken, six months later, with strange, uncontrollable new "armpowers" that have orphaned thousands, and on the run from the secret death squads of two different governments — but hey, it beats lying awake at night worrying about Inventory Reports, amirite?

You're in a peaceful forest, your senses taking in everything: golden sunlight, birdsong, tiny bugs nipping at your ears, fresh pine needles, there's the bugs again, SLAP! Ah...peace...bird chirps, faint whisp of cookout smoke, NOPE! BUGTOWN AGAIN, A CURSE UPON GOD AND HIS JOKE OF A CREATION FOR MAKING THIS ABOMINABLE TINY MONSTROSITY TO TORMENT ALL YOUR WAKING DAYS!

...I mean...*om?*

The rent is getting jacked up on your Happy Place, jacked up on your Happy Place, jacked up on your Happy Place...

You are in a rowboat on a perfect, clear pond, fishing pole in hand, and not a care in the world. And then, at approximately 25,000 miles per hour, a red-hot meteorite comes hurtling out of the atmosphere, right at you...and, barely misses, causing a huge splash and you're like, "Come ON— I **just** changed shirts!"

You're literally on top of the world, atop a majestic peak you've just climbed, a heartstopping view in every direction. Tiny puffs of smoke in the distance remind you: Did I leave the gas on? No, ridiculous, of course you turned it off. Didn't you? You did, so just relax and take in the *screeching faraway sirens trying to put out the flames*, and take a deep breath in—*inhalation being the*

DINAPOLI

#1 cause of death in fires.

Your Happy Place is being replaced by a Gap Kids, Gap Kids, Gap Kids...

—*Rob Kutner*

THE NON-APOLOGY APOLOGY OF SOCRATES.

How you, O Athenians, have been affected by my words, I cannot tell; but if I have offended anyone for the things I am supposed to have said, I would then in that case be sorry.

I dare say that some one among you will reply, "Yes, Socrates, but did you not, in a recent tweet, specifically refer to some of the participants in the recent Olympic games as 'vizzies,' a term that some in the Barbarian community consider highly insulting, itself being unflattering slang for 'Visigoth?' Tell us, Socrates what you tweeted, which was heavily ratio'd, and whether you regret your words, and also whether you think a public stoning is appropriate."

Now I regard this as a fair challenge, and I wish to acknowledge fault where such acknowledgment is appropriate, if fault there was. And so, let me be clear: if anyone was left with the impression that I was disrespectful to the Barbarians, then I deeply regret them having that impression.

The Barbarians have made many important contributions to civilization, not least in inventing new methods of beheading and flaying people in lots of unexpected ways. And the Tartars alone deserve a whole lot of credit for their sauce, without which fishsticks would be inedible.

Since the time I tweeted my lighthearted observation about the "vizzy discus hurlers from Phoenecia," however, I have learned that "Barbarian" itself is an umbrella term, and may refer to Goths, Visigoths, and even some fans of the metal bands of Carthage. I did not know this when I made my little joke, but I know it now, and I regret that I do.

I do think it is fair to acknowledge that there is some ambiguity around the term "vizzy," and a wise man may acknowledge the shortcomings in his own knowledge, and still be accorded wise. For is it not true that some Visigoths themselves have attempted to "reclaim" the word 'vizzy,' just as some of you, O Athenians, have re-appropriated the word "Ath-hole?" I can tell you that there was a time when this appellation was not exactly a compliment, especially when it was being bellowed at you by a bunch of very large Spartans with spears and a band of trained lions.

It is also worth acknowledging that many of my Visigoth friends use the word "vizzy" among themselves with some abandon, like when Meletus came back from the baths last week with his hair all weird, and Lycon (whose mother is Visigothian) said, "Mel, you are a hot vizzy mess." It was hard for a casual observer, as I describe myself, to ascertain that Lycon was reclaiming a pejorative

BOB DYLAN AND THE SONG ABOUT AN ARMADILLO

"TEXAS, YOU GOT A ROLLING THUNDER PEST."

(TO THE TUNE OF ISIS*)
* NOT THE TERRORISTS

♪ ♪

THE ARMADILLO IS A CREATURE
WHO MAKES ITSELF KNOWN
BY CREEPIN' IN YOUR GARDEN
FROM MIDNIGHT TIL DAWN.

♪ ♪

IT FLIPS ALL THE SOIL,
ROOTS OUT ALL THE WORMS
IT'D TURN OVER YOUR CAR
IF IT WANTED TO, YEA!
(HARMONICA SOLO)

"Everything about this hurts."

term, rather than just messing around.

And so, Meletus, let me ask you this: What does it mean to be sorry?

Meletus: *It means that you take responsibility for the way your words may have caused harm to others.*

But Meletus, why should we care what effect our words have on those who are not ourselves? Is it not all about us?

Meletus: *You should care because you don't want to come off like a total Athhole, Socrates. Because you want to do your best to treat your fellow-citizen with love. You don't want people to go home with weird hair AND sorry that they ran into you.*

Very well then, Meletus. Let us agree: Love means always having to say you're sorry.

Meletus: *Is that what we're agreeing? Sometimes you just say stuff. Does this mean you're actually sorry? Or what?*

Meletus, it is through knowing you that I have truly come to understand the definition of sorrow.

O men of Athens: if, as a result of the words I am supposed to have said, offense might have been taken, I would ask you all to consider my Apology carefully for what could, upon further examination, resemble indications of regret.

The unexamined apology is not worth giving.

—Jennifer Finney Boylan

BESTSELLERS.

The 4-Hour Shower
A Slightly Fabulous You
The 19 Steps to Achieving the 8 Steps that will Lead to the 37 Steps to Personal Fulfillment, Romantic Satisfaction, Professional Success, Financial Freedom, and Also, Unfortunately, Horrifically Bad Breath
So You Want to Be Me, Huh? Good Luck.
The Power of Having a Shit-Ton of Money
Awaken the Lion Within, Then Be Really Careful
Nine Steps to Stopping Yourself from Buying Books With Numbered Lists in their Title
Rich Dad, Hi Can I Have Some Money?
The World-Class Worrier
How to Fart in Public: 11 Proven Strategies
The Life-Changing Magic of a Magic Wand
Where the Fuck is My Bacon?
The NoFood Diet
Getting Things Done Until There's No More Things to Do and You Die

—Chris Dingman

CUT & RUN.

The Irish Goodbye, the French Exit… in other words, leaving a party without telling anyone. Everyone is occupied elsewhere, so you slip out.

That is child's play. The *real* trick is leaving an event when you're engaged in a one-on-one conversation. My strategy, the People Pleaser's Adieu, is simple: let the other person decide when it's over. I don't have to be honest, or hurt someone's feelings. There's no potential that

I'll overstay or understay my welcome. I linger, waiting for the other person to release me. It's a reliable system. It's only backfired once.

Two years ago, I visited a house in North Hollywood to see about renting a spare room. Both roommates worked from home; one sold junk on eBay—junk that was stacked throughout the living room—and the other was a dog-sitter. Not just any dog-sitter, she explained, but a sitter for the pets of B-level actors.

So the sitter had a least six B-level canines in her care the night I visited, which you'd think would be adorable: I'd enter this prospective home and be greeted by a tornado of fur and affection. It'd be the perfect ruse to lure me into paying $850 for a room currently painted lime green.

Except that I don't *love* dogs. I realize that's one of the most objectionable things a person can say. I don't hate dogs, but I don't love them either. If I wasn't so concerned with people's opinions of me, I'd start dropping this truth bomb as a guaranteed conversation-ender.

At the North Hollywood ~~kennel~~ house, the sitter walked me outside, where the dogs were currently penned. She pointed to a tiny, rowdy Pomeranian. "This little guy," she said, "is a biter." Then, the sitter opened the gate. And then, to her surprise, the biter bit me.

This should have been the excuse I was waiting for.

Did I dropkick Cujo and book it out of there? No. Did I politely decline her offer of roommate-ship and calmly drive to the nearest Urgent Care? Also no. Did I at least accept an adhesive bandage for my bleeding ankle? She didn't offer — and even if she had, I would've said no. I didn't want to be an inconvenience.

No, instead, I limped into the living room and had a 20-minute conversation with this person I knew would never be my roommate, internally resigning myself to a lonely, painful life with rabies.

Partings are still a struggle for me, but that day (and that dog) taught me an important lesson: the best exit strategy is uncontrollable bleeding…or, as I now call it, The Pomeranian Exit.

—Lydia Oxenham

HOW THANKFUL AM I?

"Write a thank you note within three weeks" thankful

"Have my kid draw something with crayons for you" thankful

"Really listen to you" thankful

"Pretend to listen to your significant other" thankful

"Send you a basket of bran mini muffins" thankful

"Send you a basket of chocolate full-sized muffins" thankful

"Wear that chunky wooden bead bracelet you gave me" thankful

"Pretend you weren't regifting a chunky wooden bead bracelet you got from your significant other" thankful

I'M A KANGAROO
JOEDATOR
"Your résumé is impressive."

THE DOG CAN'T CATCH IT, BUT LEAVES IT KINDA STARTLED, IT'LL BE BACK IN AN HOUR TO FINISH WHAT IT STARTED.
BOING!
SNIFF
IN THE MORNIN' WHEN YOU RISE, YOUR YARD'S A DISASTER, YOU SPEND ALL THE DAY CLEANIN' UP THE WRECKAGE.
A MAN IN A TRUCK APPROACHES WITH A GRIN, YOU KNOW RIGHT AWAY HE IS NOT ORDINARY. HE SAID "ARE YOU LOOKIN' FOR SOMETHIN' EASY TO CATCH?" YOU SAY YOU GOT SOME MONEY, HE SAYS "THAT AIN'T NECESSARY."
PEST CONTROL
HE SAYS, "YOU CAN'T TRAP THAT MAMMAL, IT IS JUST TOO CRAFTY." YOU SAY THAT'S THE WORST NEWS THAT YOU EVER HEARD.
NO CAN DILLO.

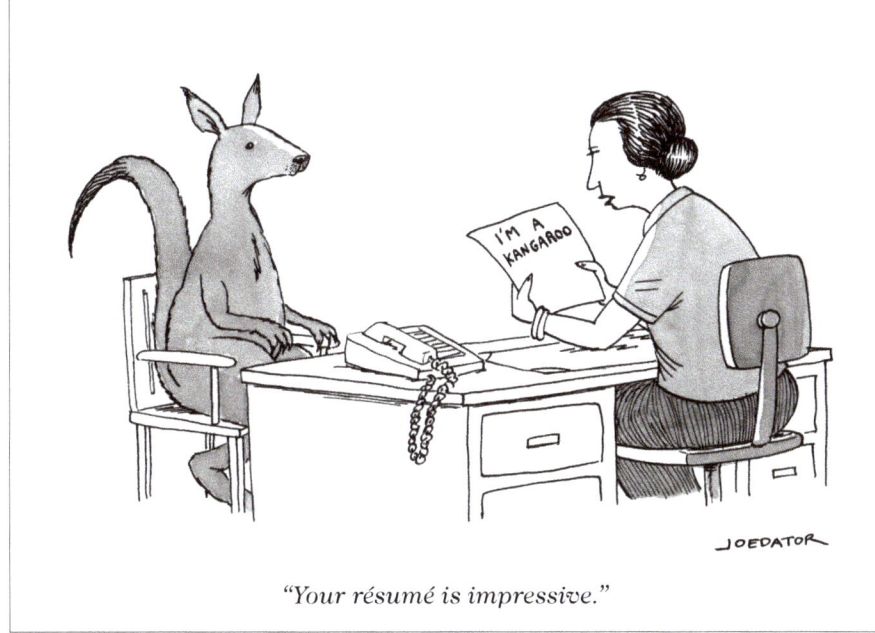

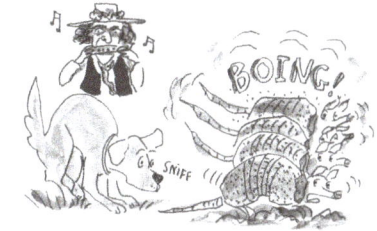

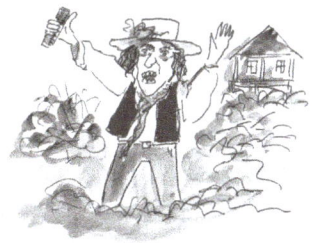

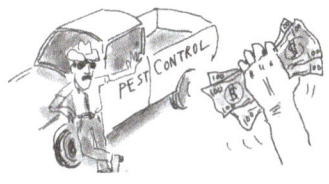

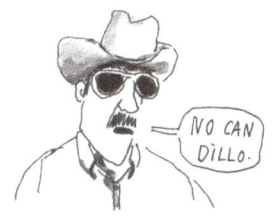

HE SAYS, "YOU GOTTA SHOOT IT."
BUT YOU'RE NOT THAT KIND OF PERSON.

SO YOU SAY A QUICK PRAYER
AND FORGET IT ALL FOR NOW.

ARMADILLO, OH, ARMADILLO
I GUESS YOU HAVE WON,
IN YOUR CRAZY GRAY ARMOR
YOU'RE GONNA HAVE YOUR FUN.

I'M THINKIN' ABOUT CRITTERS,
I'M THINKIN' ABOUT VARMINTS,
I'M THINKIN' ABOUT
   ARMADILLOS,
HOW THEY ARE SO ELUSIVE.

"Why don't you try picking on someone ten times your size?"

"Return that mystery book I borrowed from you six months ago" thankful

"Not spoil the ending to the self-help book you borrowed from me six months ago" thankful

"Buy you a Starbucks gift card" thankful

"Buy you a gift card to the really good coffee place where you caught your significant other kissing the barista" thankful

"Visit your newborn nephew with you" thankful

"Visit your newly hired divorce attorney with you" thankful

"Let you crash on my couch for a couple weeks" thankful

"Drive you to the airport" thankful

"Thankful I'm not you" thankful

—*Sheryl Zohn*

JUGS OF PEE, THE PERFECT TOSSABLE FOR REVENGE APPLICATIONS.

Peeing in jugs is a time-honored tradition of long-haul truckers, addled tycoons and the revenge-minded. I will be focusing on the latter.

Pee is naturally stinky and, when captured in a plastic jug, makes the perfect tossable for revenge applications. A basement shelf or bedroom closet can easily hold a month's worth of pee, even with the recommended one inch of clearance between jugs. A standard padlock can prevent accidental discoveries by friends and family, which never go well.

Pee should be stored between 62 and 70 degrees Fahrenheit, away from direct sunlight. Leakage should not be a problem with modern jug construction, although it is recommended that you look for a jug with a recycling code #2 (HDPE) or #1 (PET).

Why am I storing so much pee? you might ask. Because when an opportunity for revenge arises, you won't have time to produce the volume of pee necessary for the job. You will want one or more jugs of pee on hand for immediate tossing. And if, like me, the list of people upon whom you wish to exact revenge runs into two pages, you'll need several dozen jugs in your arsenal.

Tossing jugs of pee is a skill and should be practiced. Your first throw should never be at a revengee. So much could go wrong! Practice with a mannequin, scarecrow or other human substitute, preferably in a remote area with no witnesses. Novice tossers should be able to master the fundamentals in about six weeks.

Thrown jugs should be approximately half-full for maximum burst and spray upon deployment. Keep all your stock filled to the same level to ensure predictable performance. Remember, you're not aiming at the revengee, but at the ground in front of him/her. With the right toss, pee should spray impressively all over the revengee such that he/she screams "My God! What was that, pee?!"

Wear black. Run away.

—K. A. Polzin

WE HOPE YOU LIKE NEW NUMBERS!

We at the Mathematics Association are thrilled it's our 250th anniversary. To celebrate we are releasing brand new numbers FREE to you, the fans. That's right! New and free (though if you want to pay for them we won't say no)!

Here are just a few of the new numbers, which in case you missed it are totally FREE:

- *Sebenstan*
- *Twobe*
- *Snizzletron*
- *Four**

Q: *How many numbers do you plan to release, in all?*

A: *Twobe.*

While there are risks, the choice of how to use these numbers is your own. You can divide a number by snizzletron but should only do so in a loud environment like a construction site. If you multiply by sebenstan, you'll need a quiet, secluded place like a cemetery. That's right: sebenstan and snizzletron are opposites. *Surprise!*

Some of you are no doubt wondering—can I count these numbers? The answer is, ***absolutely not***. These numbers are not countable, do not attempt to count them. You can do whatever you want with these numbers, except for this one thing.

Don't be intimidated—there are lots of ways to get started. "I'm leaving in *sebenstan* minutes," you might say. Or "I have *twobe* watches strapped to my wrist." That's impossible, that many watches would crush your wrist to pulp, but it's OK. What matters is you're trying.

In addition to the Basic Numbers mentioned above, the Mathematical Association will be releasing some Advanced Numbers. Here is a taste:

- *Oswald's Variable*
- *Shmendred*
- *Yellow Six*
- *X*

You can't expect to understand these on your first try. Don't get frustrated… but also don't be afraid to give up. Most people never really grasp the Advanced numbers, no matter how hard they think at it. All of us at the Mathematical Association understand them perfectly, but that's just how the cookie crumbles.

The best way to think about advanced numbers is through metaphor. You can think of Oswald's Variable as a train, twobe as the conductor, and Yellow Six as a young woman who some villain strapped to the railroad tracks. Oh no! Who will come to rescue the maiden? Will it be X? Shmendred? This metaphor is just what mathematicians call the "Pythagorean Theorem."

We'll stop here. You're doubtless eager to get your hands on the numbers. We've put a lot of love into their design, but it's

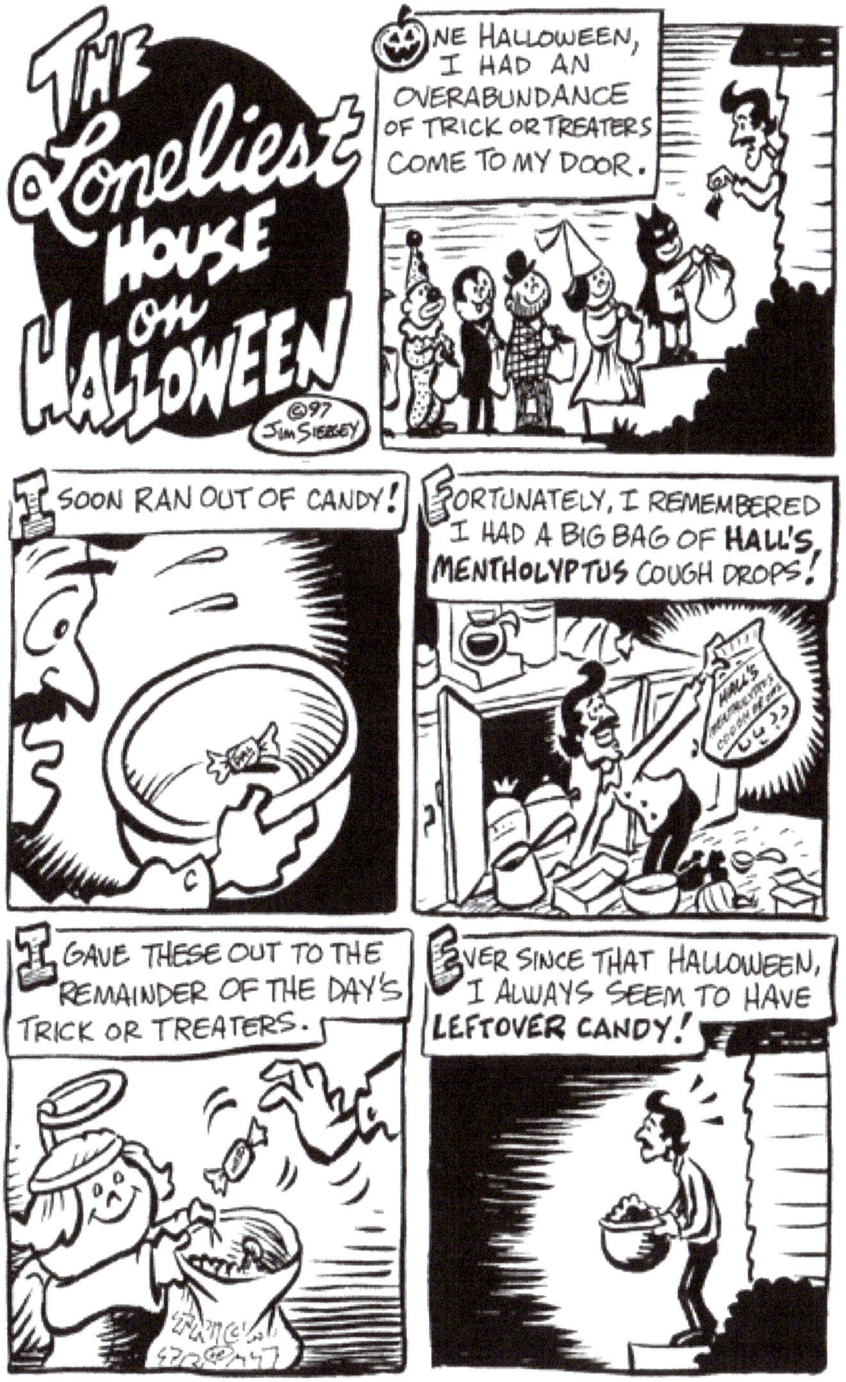

The Loneliest House on Halloween
©97
ONE HALLOWEEN, I HAD AN OVERABUNDANCE OF TRICK OR TREATERS COME TO MY DOOR.
I SOON RAN OUT OF CANDY!
FORTUNATELY, I REMEMBERED I HAD A BIG BAG OF HALL'S MENTHOLYPTUS COUGH DROPS!
HALL'S
I GAVE THESE OUT TO THE REMAINDER OF THE DAY'S TRICK OR TREATERS.
EVER SINCE THAT HALLOWEEN, I ALWAYS SEEM TO HAVE LEFTOVER CANDY!

*This isn't the old four—it's a brand new four. The new four is twice as long, which is how we originally intended it. It's spelled the same way, but pronounced *ffoouurr.*

STAN MACK'S CHRONICLES

SMELL THAT WISTERIA! YOU LIVE IN SUCH A QUAINT AND PEACEFUL NEIGHBORHOOD.
IT'S DECEPTIVE. ON THIS SPOT IN 1777, THEY FOUGHT THE FAMOUS BATTLE OF SHAY'S CORNERS.
A BLOODY CONFRONTATION THAT LEFT BODIES STREWN ACROSS THE FIELD OF BATTLE.
ICE CREAM
I BELIEVE THAT WHAT LURKS BENEATH RISES WITH EVERY GENERATION.
IN THAT HOUSE, A MAN SMOTHERED HIS WIFE IN THE LAUNDRY ROOM AND RAN OFF WITH THE NANNY.
DEAD END
THE GUY NEXT DOOR WAS CHASING SQUIRRELS WITH A BB GUN WHEN HIS PACEMAKER GAVE OUT.
PRESS
ON THAT CORNER, THE WOMAN'S FOUR HUSBANDS ALL DIED ODDLY. AND EACH TIME, SHE ADDED AN EXTENSION ONTO HER HOUSE.
SLOW
HI, MOMMY.
HELLO, SWEETHEART.
HI, DADDY.
HOW WAS CAMP TODAY, BUDDY?
HEY KID, BEWARE! THE FRAGRANCE OF WISTERIA CLOAKS MISCHIEF AND MAYHEM.
?
© 2019 stanmack

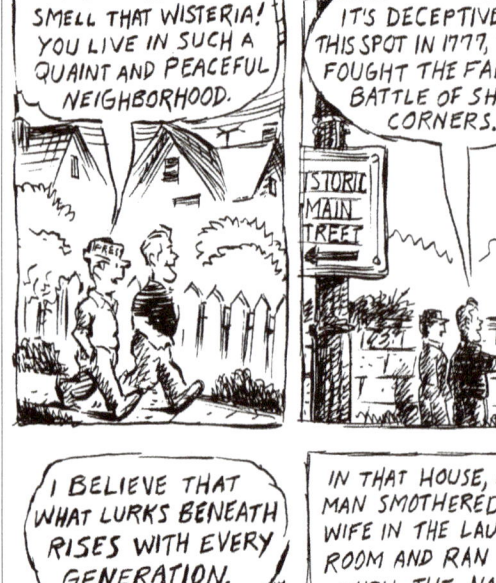

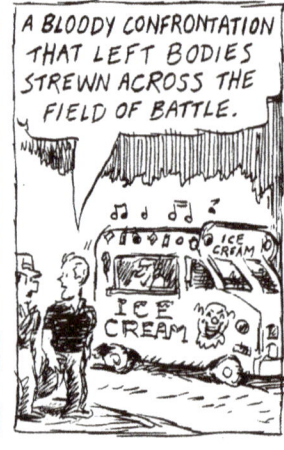

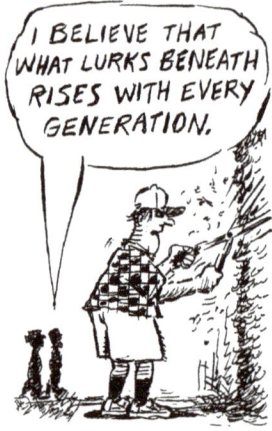

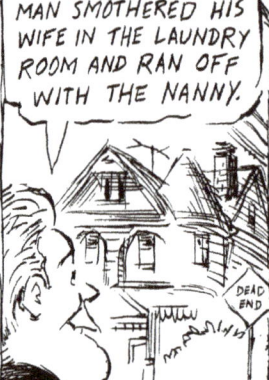

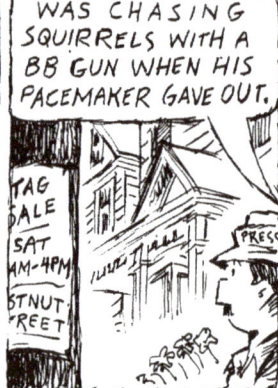

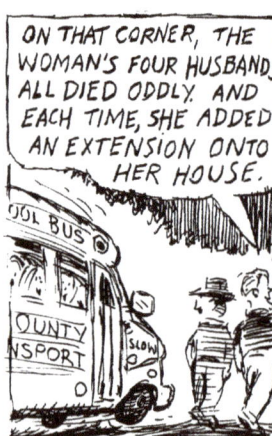

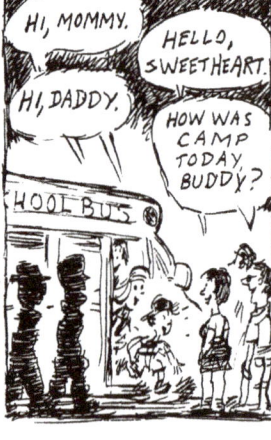

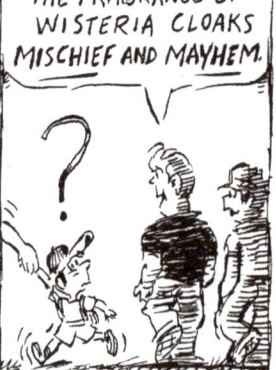

time to let go.

One last thing. We lied. These numbers are completely FREE but only for a limited time. Or, more to the point, they are not free at all. The limited time has passed already, just twobe moments ago. You missed it. But join the Mathematical Association now and you get FREE and unrestricted access to all these numbers—and *more*.

Join today!

—Michael Pershan

THE MIRROR.

A middle-aged man in a business suit is about to walk out of his apartment. He reaches toward the doorknob, then halts abruptly. There is panic on his face. He tries again and again, but he can't bring himself to touch the doorknob.

He checks his pockets, his hair, his shoelaces, making sure everything is in order. Something is wrong. He doesn't know what, but he simply can't leave the room until he figures it out.

He turns around and starts checking and straightening everything in sight. But still something is very wrong. Something he can't identify.

Finally he turns toward the mirror over his bureau. Once again he checks pockets, hair, shoelaces. He checks his wallet, his zipper, his tie.

Once again, he halts abruptly. He feels the tie at his collar. Looking down, he sees the tie hanging in front of his shirt. But the image of himself in the mirror has no tie.

His eyes open wide in shock as he looks from mirror to tie to mirror. It's a dull green tie, held in place by a silver-plated tie clasp. It goes well with his gray suit. But it simply doesn't appear in the mirror.

In the mirror, he himself looks the same as always. His height and build are the same. He'd recognize his face anywhere.

Everything in the mirror is the same as everything he sees on him and around him—the gray suit, the white shirt, the black shoes. Yes, that's certainly his own face, with an expression of confusion and fear.

He shuts his eyes, turns around and looks again. Still the image in the mirror is not wearing a tie.

He goes to his bed and lies down again. Then he gets up and walks to the mirror—still no tie.

He undresses, climbs back into bed, gets out of bed again and dresses again, just as before. Then he walks to the mirror—still no tie.

He starts testing the image in the mirror as if it might not be real. He moves a hand quickly, then both hands, and the head, and the hips, and a leg —faster, and faster. The image in the mirror falls at the very same time he falls.

He gets up, smooths out his clothes, clenches and unclenches his fists several times.

Then he checks his watch, takes a deep breath, and stares again at his image in the mirror.

Finally, he takes his tie off, hangs it with his other ties in the closet, calmly walks to the door, turns the doorknob, and enters the world.

—Richard Seltzer B

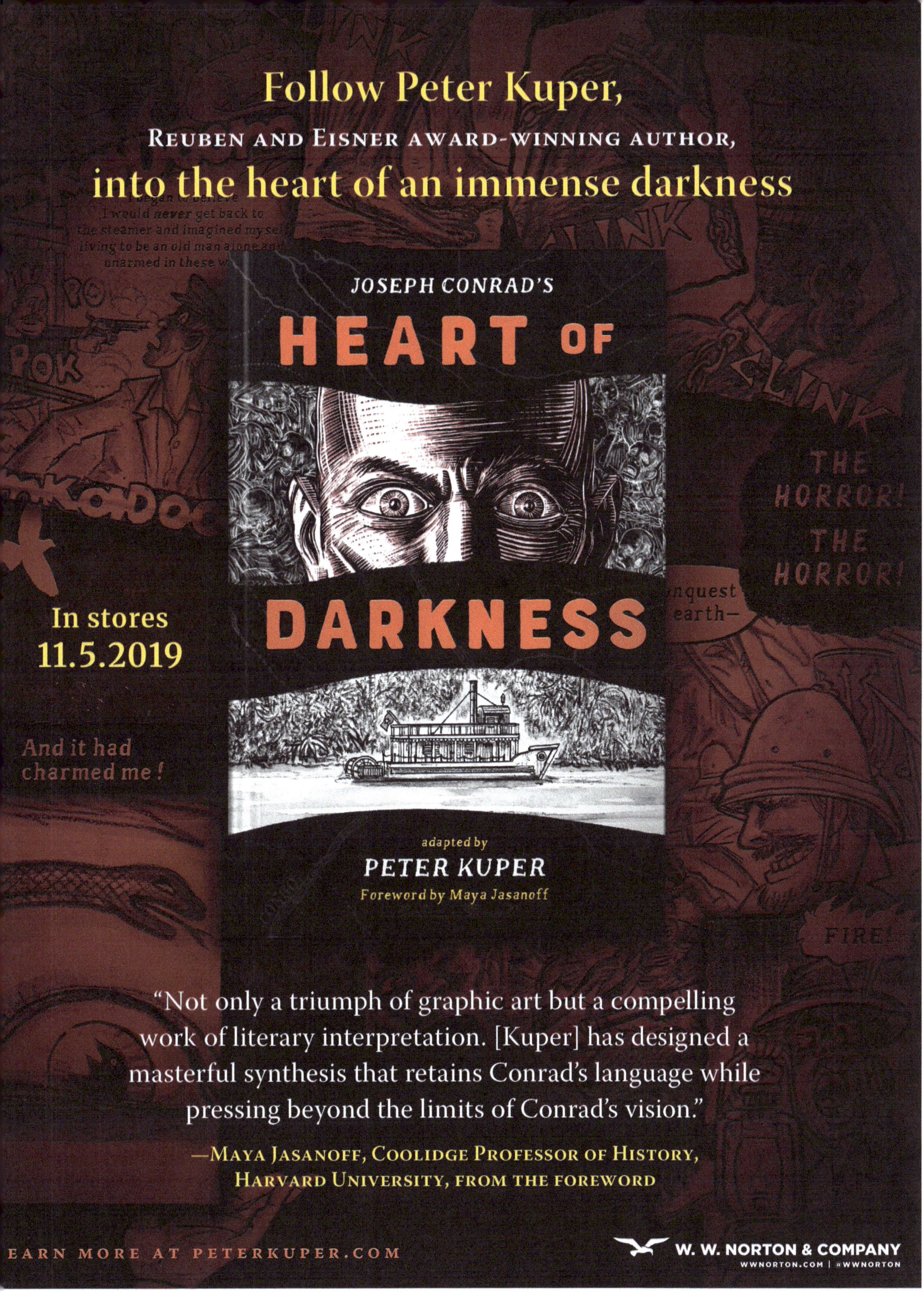

Follow Peter Kuper,
Reuben and Eisner award-winning author,
into the heart of an immense darkness
JOSEPH CONRAD'S
HEART OF DARKNESS
adapted by
PETER KUPER
Foreword by Maya Jasanoff
In stores 11.5.2019
And it had charmed me!
THE HORROR! THE HORROR!
CLINK
FIRE!
"Not only a triumph of graphic art but a compelling work of literary interpretation. [Kuper] has designed a masterful synthesis that retains Conrad's language while pressing beyond the limits of Conrad's vision."
—Maya Jasanoff, Coolidge Professor of History, Harvard University, from the foreword
EARN MORE AT PETERKUPER.COM
W. W. NORTON & COMPANY
WWNORTON.COM | @WWNORTON

What if every cheesy Christmas movie ever made was mashed up into one book ... and you controlled the plot?

Find out this holiday season!

"AN INSTANT CLASSIC"

"A REVELATION"

"AN ABSOLUTE TOUR DE FORCE"

BUILD YOUR OWN
CHRISTMAS
MOVIE ROMANCE
Pick Your Plot, Meet Your Man, and Create the Holiday Love Story of a Lifetime
RIANE KONC

These are just some of the things we wish critics would say about *Build Your Own Christmas Movie Romance.*

ULYSSES PRESS

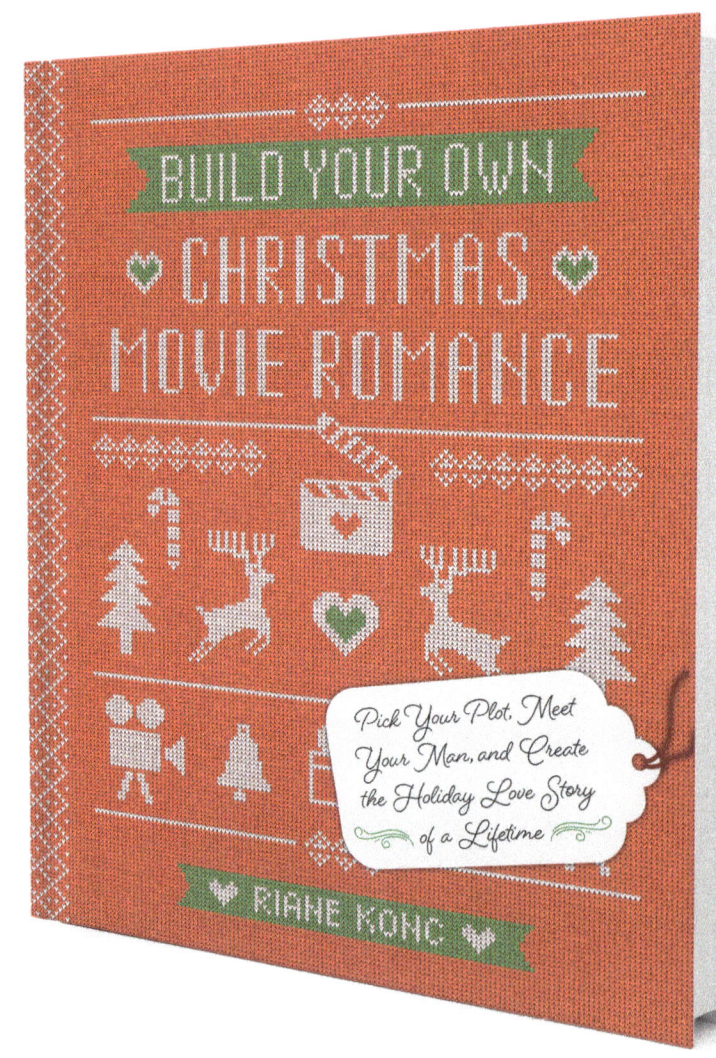

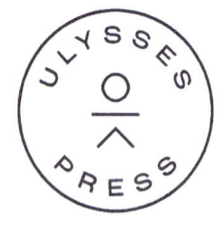

Available October 2019

BY JUSTIN COURTER

BARELY CREDIBLE

Hulk just read AARP Magazine *and, you know what? Hulk really enjoy it*

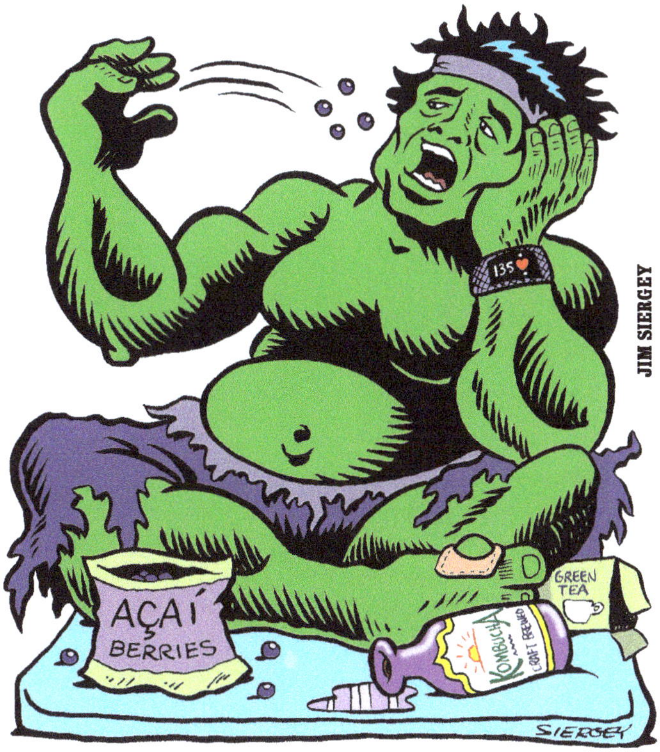

135
AÇAÍ BERRIES
GREEN TEA
KOMBUCHA
CRAFT BREWED
SIERGEY

JIM SIERGEY

Month ago, Hulk had mild heart attack. Doctor say Hulk have high blood pressure, from anger-management problem. That make Hulk mad, SMASH desk. Doctor say, see? Hulk grudgingly admit doctor have point. Doctor tell Hulk take it easy because of "serious risk of cardiac arrest."

This first time Hulk ever use quote-fingers.

List of foods Hulk must avoid is long. Hulk had no idea deli meat, frozen pizza, canned soups contain so much salt! Salt absolute bitch for Hulk's hypertension. Salt Hulk's new arch enemy!

Hulk go to grocery store and SMASH evil deli counter! SMASH shelves of canned soup! Was about to start on frozen foods, but women screaming, kids crying. Puny manager beg Hulk to stop. Police cars, helicopters, tear gas. Hulk run away and hide, feel terrible about whole mess. Hulk 57, not kid! When Hulk grow up?

Just working through bad news, Hulk guess. Feelings of mortality. All Hulk not done, dreams not accomplished by Hulk.

Hulk not feel like SMASHING much since then. Old softball injury flared up again—Hulk no raise right arm over head without excruciating pain. Hulk taking, like, 300 Advils/day, now freaking out about liver cancer.

Hulk can't SMASH full-force now. And heart not in it, to tell truth. Now and then, to remind Hulk still strongest one there is, Hulk give a little half-SMASH. Hope no one notice Hulk wincing, how feeble nowadays are the SMASHES.

And Hulk rarely get smashed now either. Hulk angry drunk—no surprise—which mean blood pressure go up, elevated risk of stroke. So Hulk limit self to two beers, max. Who want brain damage? Not Hulk.

Hulk brain not so great in first place. Hulk first read about CTE, mouth go dry, almost shit self right there. All time Hulk used head to SMASH bad guys. If anyone know about CTE back then, no tell Hulk. Hulk not even have big NFL salary to fall back on—all just volunteer work!

Hulk suddenly understand phrase "midlife crisis." Hulk question *everything*.

Hulk mean, what the shit!? Hulk no even have health insurance! Hulk *need* job with benefits. Hulk been putting off prostate exam, Hulk worry about bone density...Next SMASH could be Hulk's own femur!

Is not so simple—as pencil-neck Doctor make it sound—for Hulk to "take it easy." For Hulk, easy is hard. Not want to become like Banner. Baby Bruce. Timid. Afraid of anger, afraid of frozen pizza, afraid of everything. That not real living.

But Hulk also not want to wind up on life-support, surrounded by Avengers saying, "Hulk stupid. Hulk not take care of self."

What Hulk supposed to do? Work as bouncer? Practice mindfulness meditation? Do yoga? Work in tollbooth? Kinda comedown for strongest one there is!

Sometimes Hulk wish Bruce Banner never met gamma rays. Is Hulk saying he wish he never born? Hulk feel that way sometimes. Hulk not mean to be downer, Hulk figure out eventually, but...What Hulk trying say?...

Kermit Frog right: It not easy being green. But *middle-aged* even worse. **B**

JUSTIN COURTER *(@JustinCourter) has written three books, including* **Skunk: A Love Story***. He lives in New York City.*

FRIENDLY ADVICE
BY JENNIFER KIM
CITY LIFE
Are you ready for Life in the Big City? Probably not

Hey Kid,

Welcome to the big city. You might've noticed that I'm wearing a leather jacket and holding a rusted wrench. And I am. Good job for noticing. This is the big, bad city and you have to be able to notice things here.

This place ain't soft. There aren't any babies riding bicycles around eating baby-shaped ice cream and singing lullabies to smaller babies or some shit. Here in this lawless, concrete jungle, things are different.

In the big city, when you ask for directions, people will try to trick you. I'd say a solid nine times out of ten, they will give you directions to the opposite place of where you're going. If you want to go south, they'll point you north. If you want to get some good coffee, they'll send you to the worst coffee joint in all of town. If you want to go get a haircut, they'll send you to Tony, the wig guy. I've made that mistake a couple times, so be careful.

In the big city, when you want to make friends, there's a fifty-fifty chance that you will join a gang by mistake. And they won't be dancing and singing songs like in *West Side Story*, unless it's the "Broadway Babies" which is the gang made up of all failed musical theater actors. They're pretty talented.

In the big city, when you pass by a bunch of business guys shaking hands, it's not a fun little game they're doing where you can just jump in and shake hands with everyone like it's no big deal. They get pretty irked because it's some kind of "exclusive" thing they're doing. Who wants to be part of that club anyway? Not me. Whatever.

In the big city, when you see a man walking down the street holding a jug of milk, he isn't the milkman. He won't smile, wave at you, or come up to you asking how your morning is or how many bottles of milk you want. Instead, he'll smile, wave at you, and come up to you and tell you crazy stories about how the whole city is being slowly overrun by intelligent lizards. Sometimes, he'll ask you if you want some milk, but I wouldn't take it if I were you.

In the big city, nobody knows your name. At first, your feelings might be hurt about it. But then, you realize this can be a good thing. You can reinvent yourself and you can be whoever you want to be. You can be Alfred, Durkes, or Frank. But those are the only options.

In the big city, you might find that teenagers are kind of mean to you. You might find yourself walking by a group of kids hanging around at the 7-Eleven and they call you "Loserface" or "Mr. Fatty McGee." You'll scoff in front of them, but then later when you're home alone, you'd be surprised to find that even though you thought it wouldn't get to you, it does. "Mr. Fatty McGee" in particular. Where did they even learn that one? Jerk school?

In the big city, when you see a dog tied to a pole outside a restaurant or something, it doesn't mean that the dog is being pressured to strip by its owners. You don't have to rescue them or help them in any way. On some occasions, you'll find that they are actually being pressured to strip. In that case, you should leave them a couple dollars or something, because they're doing some decent work there.

In the big city, when you bump into people on accident, they will get mad and ask you what your problem is. Best course of action is to be honest, because this city is real and it can handle the hard, cold truth. You can say "My problem is that I think I was never really as nice to my parents as I should've been, considering the immense sacrifices they made for me. Sorry 'bout it!" and walk off gripping your rusted, manly wrench tighter than ever.

So like I said kid, this city is bigger and scarier than anything you've experienced. I don't know if you're ready but there's only one way to find out. Good luck and when you're all settled in with work and your apartment and whatnot, let me know if you want to hang or grab a coffee or something. A big city coffee.

B

JENNIFER KIM (@kjenn32) *is a comedy writer in Los Angeles. She has contributed to places like* **McSweeney's, Points in Case,** *and* **Little Old Lady Comedy.** *It is good!*

GLENN MARSHALL

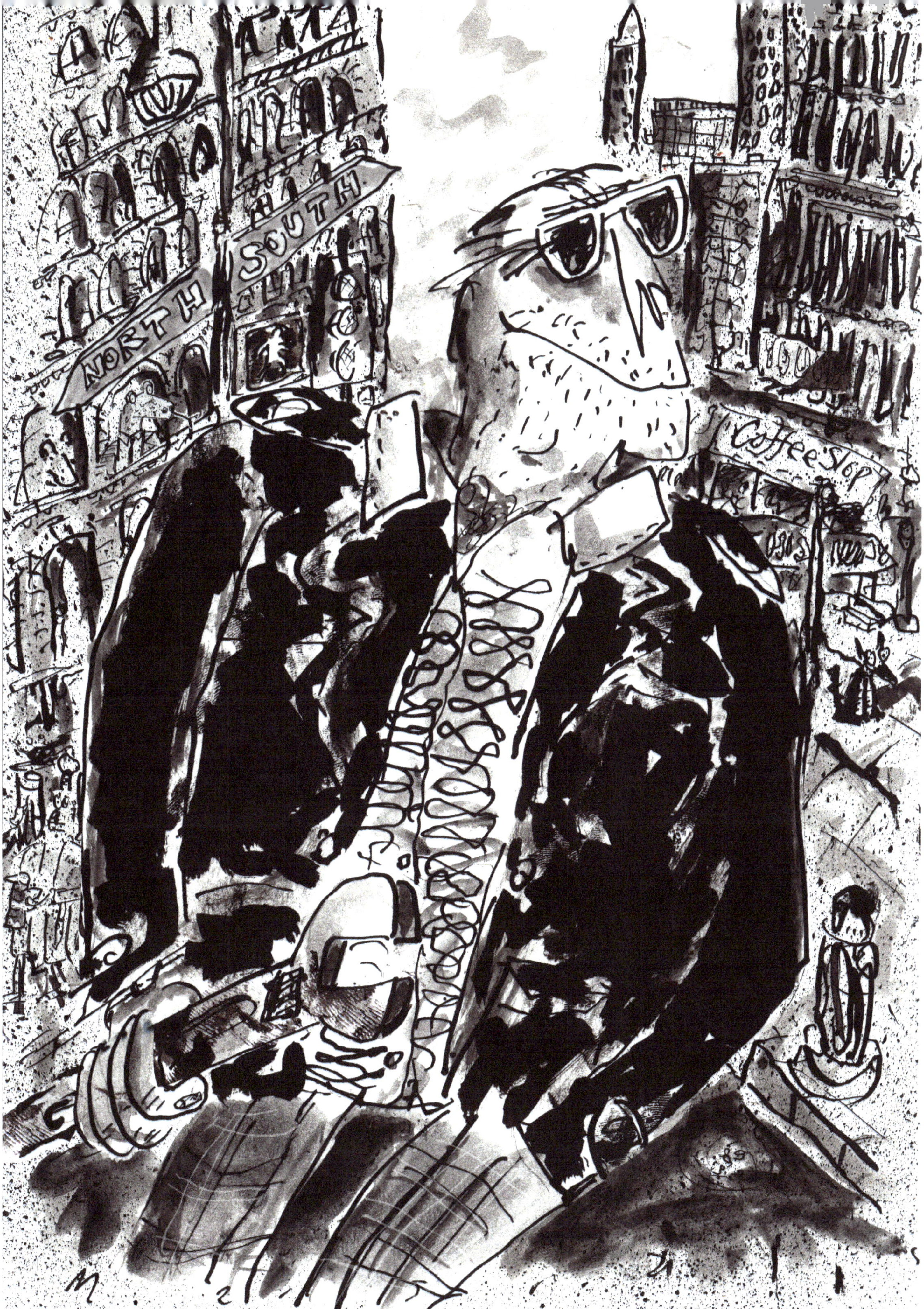

ARTS & CRAFTS
BY LOU BEACH
BLUE MASTODON
"We found her crouched behind a saber-tooth tiger made of plaster, her arms around its striped hind legs."

"OH HELL!"

"What's the matter?" I said.

"There are moths in the flour."

"What, those pantry moths?" I said, putting down the morning paper.

Gina looked at me over the tops of her glasses. "Yeah, not the ones that eat our sweaters," she said. "I'm dumping the flour."

"Don't, it's no big deal," I said, "they don't carry disease. You pluck the little beasties out, sift the flour, whatever. I hate wasting food."

"Yeah, fine, you eat it then. I won't touch it. I'm going to the market after work for some more flour. This is spoiled."

"You're spoiled," I said.

She wanted to be annoyed but a laugh spilled out of her.

"Spoil me some more, Victor," she said and quickly shed her jeans and panties. She still had on her apron, the one I liked, the one I called her Van Gogh, the blue one with the sunflowers. It was tied behind her, the bow spread over her ass. She leaned over the sink and braced herself against the counter. I pressed into her and she accidentally hit the switch to the garbage disposal. She didn't turn it off and the hole in the sink continued to whir and grind until we were done.

"Moths don't fuck, right? They what...procreate?" I said, zipping up.

"Moths mate, DP," she said. She turned off the disposal but didn't bother putting on her jeans.

She called me DP, her domestic partner. We'd been living together for seven years. It was still good.

I'd told her about being called a "dirty DP" as a youngster. I was a Displaced Person then, as were my mother and father. We were unable to return to our homeland when the war ended in Europe. After a long sea voyage we landed at Ellis Island, then boarded a train for Chicago, where we had a sponsor, a member of the refugee community who would vouch for us, offer assistance. He met us at the train station and tried to sell my parents a life insurance policy. I was four years old.

My mother wouldn't have thrown out the flour, I thought. She'd once described her desperation during the winter of 1941 when starving, she ate the neighbor's yellow cat; and then how in the spring of the following year she joined a hungry crowd that was armed with pistols and clubs. It hunted at the municipal zoo.

Growing up I couldn't have any pets. My mother became a vegetarian and would not watch programs about animals, left the room if one were on TV. During a vacation road trip out West she heard a wolf cry in the night and covered her ears.

Driving through the vast Western states on that last family vacation, my father would put his hand out the window and wiggle his fingers in the heated air. "I love this country," he said. "It is like an ocean," while my mother avoided looking at the occasional elk or horse in the distance.

After arriving in Los Angeles, the final destination on our vacation trip, we visited the usual tourist attractions—Hollywood Boulevard, the Pacific, Disneyland. The last stop was the La Brea Tar Pits, where a concrete mastodon stood trapped in bubbling black soup. I was transfixed by the huge

LOU BEACH *is an artist, writer, and award-winning illustrator living in Los Angeles.*

beast, and pressed my face against the chain link fence so hard that a photo from that day shows me with a crisscross pattern on my forehead and nose and cheeks; I look quilted.

"The bubbles," my mother said and looked away, crying. Something about the way they erupted on the face of the inky tar pool upset her. My father was embarrassed, afraid of sticking out, of not seeming like an American—which he most longed to be—and he gripped her elbow and tried to lead her away. She ran from him and into the small museum that adjoined the Tar Pits. We found her crouched behind a saber-tooth tiger made of plaster, her arms around its striped hind legs.

My mother was hospitalized soon after that day at the La Brea Terror Pits, as she called it. She is still being cared for, in a nice facility in Glendale, and I visit when I can, though she thinks I'm the neighbor's boy from her childhood. My father reluctantly divorced her and moved to Arizona when I finished my first year at UCLA. He loves the heat and far-off horizons, so different from the harsh winters and claustrophobic forests of Eastern Europe. He married a Mexican woman who raises dogs. He wears a cowboy hat.

I went to the market for Gina and bought flour and some other things we needed and passed the Tar Pits on the way home. I slowed for a moment and waved at the mastodons and my mother. This was the last place where she seemed whole and I believe some part of her remained here with the black water and concrete brutes. I honked the horn and drove home.

Gina was at work and I had the house to myself. I put the groceries away and tidied up the kitchen. The infested flour was still on the counter and I picked up the bag. I gave it a squeeze and a little smoke signal puffed from the folded-over top. Perhaps that's where the idea came from.

I emptied the bag into a large bowl, then added enough water to make a soupy paste. I took the morning paper from the table where I'd left it and tore the pages into strips and placed them in the bowl of paste. With pliers from a kitchen drawer I snipped some wire hangers I found in the hall closet and bent them into an armature, filling it out with pieces of cardboard held together with tape. I had a general form now and proceeded to cover it with the strips of sticky newspaper until a creature emerged. The long curved tusks proved difficult, but I was soon done and put my creation on the patio to dry in the hot sun.

I answered emails and engaged in busywork until my animal was dry and ready to paint. In the garage I found the gallon of blue paint Gina had picked out for the guest room. It was going to be the nursery but she miscarried and it went back to being a guest room, used mostly when my father came to town.

I painted the *papier-mâché* beast and left it out in the sun again to dry, then brought it into the kitchen after a while and set it on the table so it faced the door.

When Gina came home and saw it, she said: "Oh!" and touched it with one finger then picked it up and examined it carefully, turning it over and looking at it from different angles.

"Wow, DP," she said. "It's beautiful, really. A blue elephant."

"Mastodon," I said.

"Right," she said, "the tusks. But…what…why did you make it?"

I touched her face. "I hate wasting food." B

FEAR PORTUGUEXIT!
BY ALEX SCHMIDT

ACTUALLY, MY TODDLER IS PLAYING 4-D CHESS

"Trump Can Play 4-D Chess When He Wants To"
—**National Review**
"Just how many dimensions of chess is Elon Musk playing?"—**Financial Times**
"You better play 4-D chess with me like it's Minority Report. *Because it ain't that simple. It's complex."*
—Kanye West

Actually, my toddler is playing 4-D chess. You think he's eating crayons? He's actually leveraging the media. You think he's kicking your shins? He's actually controlling the narrative. Whichever level you think my Drayden is on, he's actually above it and beyond it and 100% right to shove that hot dog cart into traffic.

Actually, I do know what's best for my toddler. Because "parenting-as-usual" is in the past. My child throwing his vegetables into your hall closet is the *future*. You'll understand why soon. And if "soon" never comes? There's actually nothing more 4-D chess than that.

You've *actually* never heard of 4-D chess? Put it this way: life is a chessboard, and you're playing checkers. Meanwhile Drayden flips the whole dang board over, then shoves the chess pieces into our dachshund. Wow, you think that "sounds bad"? Sounds like you're learning The Art Of The Checkmate from a kid who can't even read yet (or can he?? (he cannot (which is all part of his master plan 😎))).

Actually, "under-parented" is the new "complex entrepreneur." Actually, my toddler's biggest wins are his "boo-boos" and "lapses" and "legally actionable Show-And-Tells." Actually yes I want a child who bangs on pastry cases. Who calls flight attendants HBO Words. Whose personal brand is "Visionary Artist" and whose chosen medium is gravel-throwing.

His other personal brand is "The Johnny Appleseed of *E. coli*." And if you think about it, any nickname from a school nurse is an achievement.

Actually, I'm actually so proud of my actual 4D Chess Grandmaster. Gosh, listen to me. Am I becoming that parent who brags every time their kid wears a Halloween costume to a state funeral? And cyberbullies *Paw Patrol* voice actors? And calls in a dirty bomb threat to The Met Gala? I'm sure every parent thinks their toddler is special and unique and an Editor-at-Large for Breitbart. But my toddler is actually all those things. And I want everyone to know it, even if they missed John Oliver's deep-dive.

Anyway enjoy the rest of your time at this playground. I'm sorry-not-sorry your kid isn't on my son's level. I remember when Drayden couldn't punt a duck, or deforest a county, or incite Portuguexit. But look at him now! It just took a little time! And a lot of permission, lobbied for by enablers!

Oh and if your kid is one of those girls over there, please make their future playground visits less shrill.

ALEX SCHMIDT (@alexschmidty) is a comedy writer, Earwolf podcaster, and **Jeopardy!** champion. His website is alexschmidty.com and his own son is a fine upstanding young cat.

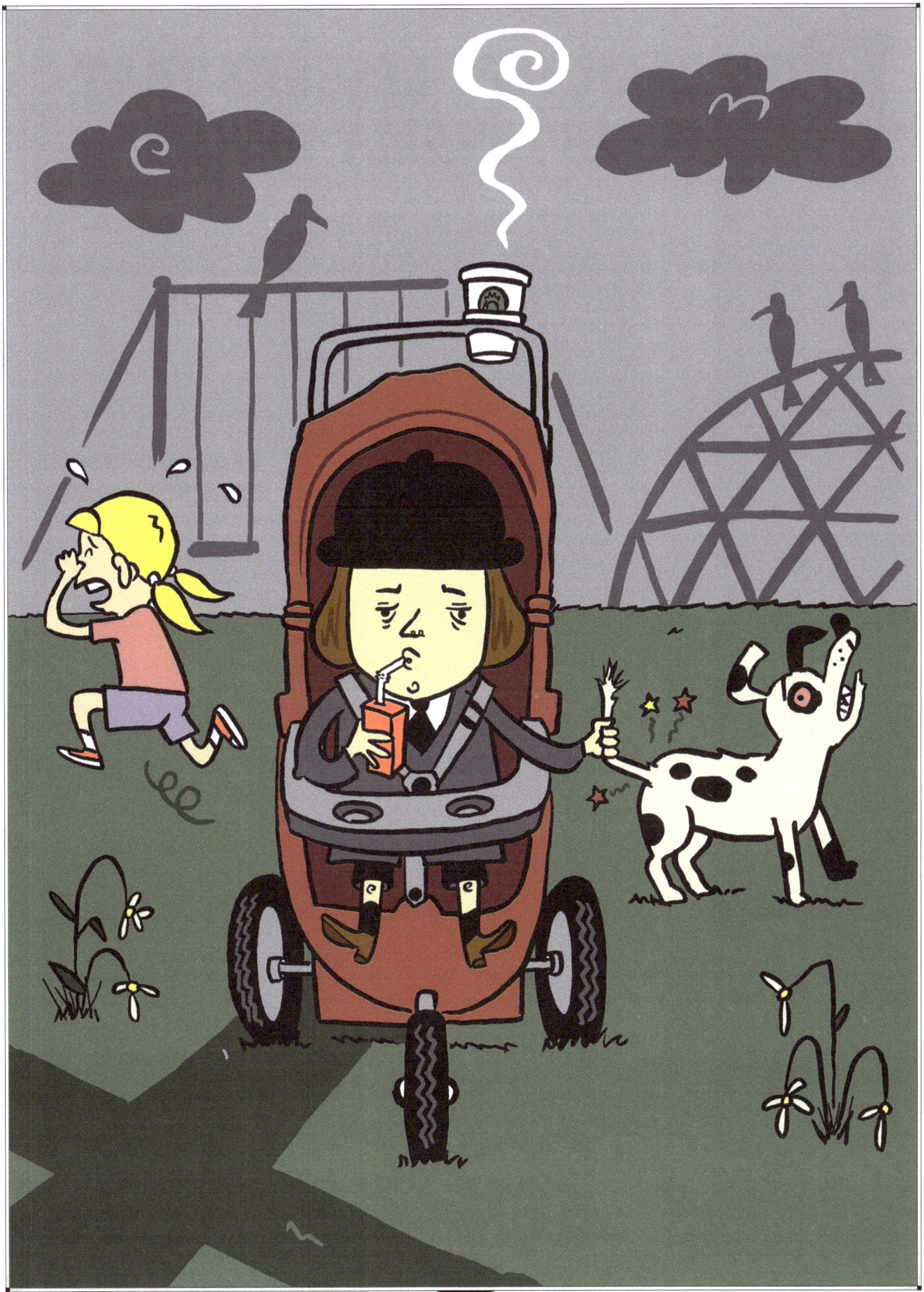

GREAT SEO
BY MEG FAVREAU

FIVE BASIC LIFE-LESSONS THAT CLUELESS TOTALLY NAILED!

MARQUES DUGGANS

If you love the classic 90s film *Clueless*, you're not alone! Lots of people clicked on this article because seeing the title of a movie they watched during their formative years gave them a pleasant burst of nostalgia. It might've been over 20 years since we first saw Cher's antics, but *Clueless* has remained a favorite film because there are so many things that the 90s classic got *so* right. So if you're so desperate to ignore your job that you want to be reminded of literally anything from a movie you once saw, look no further—this list is chock full of text and distracting gifs about the very basic life lessons *Clueless* totally got right!

1. PEOPLE WEAR CLOTHES

It's not just that Cher is obsessed with clothes in *Clueless*—literally *everybody* is wearing them. Whether you believe that people wear clothes because of personal style, temperature fluctuations, or because of a deep-seated shame of nudity that came from religion, *Clueless* totally understood that *almost all humans wear clothes*.

2. CARS GO ON THE HIGHWAY

Cher, Dionne, and Murray freaked when they accidentally moved their car onto the highway. Was it maybe because they thought cars didn't belong there? If so, they were *wrong*—cars definitely drive on the highway! Nailing that fact was just one way *Clueless* showed awesome attention to detail.

3. DURING THE DAYTIME, IT'S LIGHT OUTSIDE

Clueless's cinematographer Bill Pope made a really smart move: in order to show that it was daytime when Cher and pals were at school, they filmed the scenes during the day. Can you *imagine* if they had filmed it at night??? That would be crazy, but not as crazy as the fact that you're still skimming this article when there are literally billions of other things you could be reading on the internet!

4. HUMAN BEINGS USE LANGUAGE TO COMMUNICATE

Obviously, writer/director Amy Heckerling understands one thing about human nature: *people use language to communicate*. So here's a *Clueless* easter egg: Those noises you hear coming out of the actors mouths? They're words from the English language being strung together to convey ideas! And while some people might've thought that was just a 90s fad, they were "clueless"—language is *just as popular today!*

5. PEOPLE LIKE MOVIES (AND MOVIE CLICKBAIT!)

Perhaps the biggest thing *Clueless* got right? Understanding that people enjoy movies. So instead of writing the story of *Clueless* on a truly *epic* scroll, or whispering it to a friendly snail, Heckerling made it into a film, a format that allowed the story to be consumed by millions of people, instead of a small cabal of scroll lovers or one invertebrate. *Genius!* Plus, by making such a totally awesome movie, Heckerling was able to inspire years of insipid clickbait for a world where the pace of technology has vastly outstripped the pace of our brain's evolution, leading us all to spend our time skimming anything that can give us a momentary zing of pleasure, even if we recognize on a very deep level that it's a complete and utter waste of this, our one, very finite, very precious human life.

But are we going to stop?

In the immortal words of Cher: *As if!*

MEG FAVREAU (@megfavreau) *lives in Los Angeles, where she writes for animated series and regularly dresses up as a giant eye. You can see more from her at* megfavreau.com.

This advertisement is authorised by Scarfolk Council

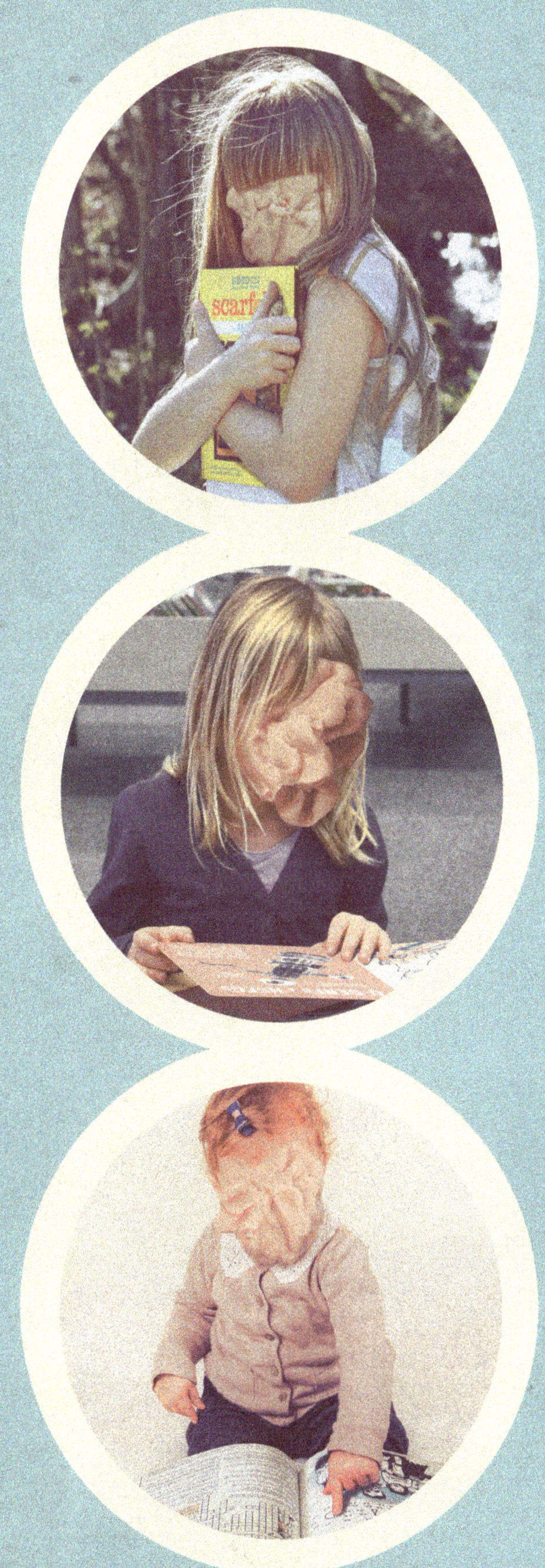

"Scarfolk might be the most satisfying bit of sustained satire I've encountered since, well, The Onion"

- Dangerous Minds

"Meticulously detailed and impressively creepy"

- Atlas Obscura

"We've never had to deal with a more glaring example"

- Case CR98-1: Contravention of the Psychological Torture Act. New York County Court Files

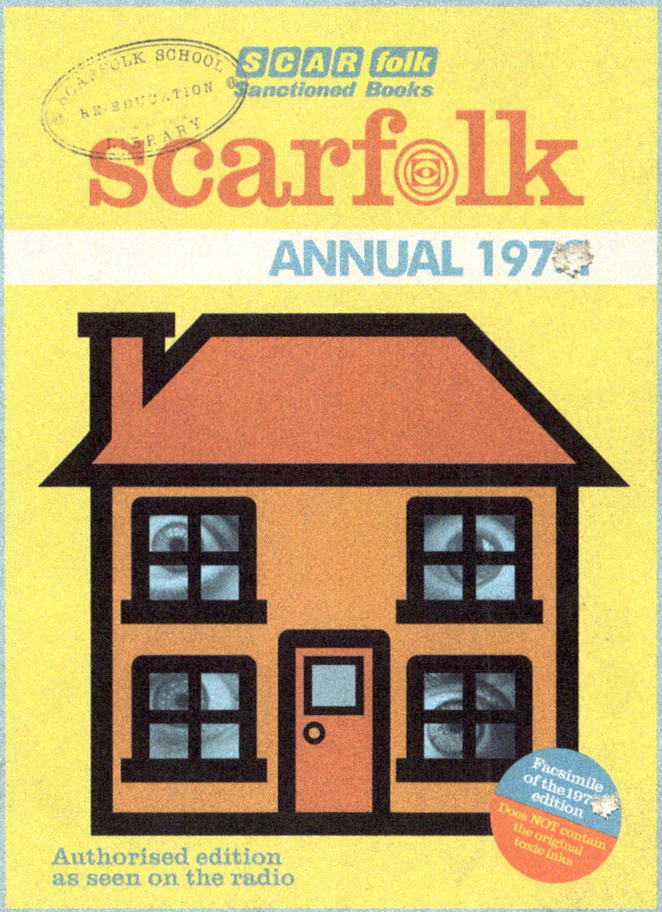
SCAR folk
Sanctioned Books
scarfolk
ANNUAL 197
Facsimile of the 197 edition
Does NOT contain the original toxic inks
Authorised edition as seen on the radio

Available from:

Amazon, Barnes & Noble, Indiebound, Books-A-Million & others

For more information please re-read

Tele-Ween

This isn't just a cynical candy grab, Mrs. Gorbowski.

Hello, is this Eileen Gorbowski of 44 Leighton Street? Hi, Mrs. Gorbowski, this is Ted Lewis, from around the corner at 19 Alder Lane. Happy Halloween! I'm calling to say Trick-or-treat! Well, many of us kids prefer to trick-or-treat by phone now because it's more efficient. You can hit a lot more houses if you're not doing all the walking. But I do take this seriously—I'm wearing a ghost costume right now. It's a premium-quality costume, lots of gauzy white fabric. Can you visualize it? And I'm wearing a mask with a scary ghost face. That's why I sound slightly muffled but I hope you'll agree it's worth it. *Boo!* Yes, I said "Boo!" That's the traditional ghost catchphrase. You have to imagine me in the ghost costume, saying it on your front porch. Do you have that picture in your mind? Then you've now gotten the full effect! So, do you have candy for trick-or-treaters this year? Oh, the Fun Size Snickers bars? Terrific, that's a wonderful candy. Would you be able to reserve a few of those for me? Yes, well, I'll need you to mail them. I realize it's an inconvenience. Regular Priority Mail would be fine, though if you were moved to opt for Express Mail due to my great overall presentation, that's up to you! Did you write down my address? It's 19 Alder Lane. Lewis, L-E-W-I-S. If you could email the tracking number that would be appreciated. Last year when I was making my calls dressed as a robot, several people promised to send me candy that never arrived. Did I call you last Halloween? I didn't? Well, I didn't intentionally overlook you. I often have quite lengthy calls to ensure a top-quality experience, and there are always some people I can't get to. But I assure you my robot costume was quite impressive: classic retro mid-century futuristic, with lights and dials and the big silvery parts. Can you visualize the robot costume? I don't know whether that additional visualization is worth more candy—that's a question for you and your conscience.

You've got another call coming in? Yes, I'll hold.

Yes, I'm still here. Another phone trick-or-treater? Oh, Arthur Findley from Groton Street. Yes, I know Arthur from school. Confidentially, I don't think Arthur takes this as seriously as I do. What did he say he was wearing? Oh, the Batman costume, right. I've heard from his sister that when he does his trick-or-treat phone calls, he doesn't even put on the mask because it gets irritating and he worries that it will exacerbate his acne. Naturally I'm sympathetic, but to me if it's a choice between doing Halloween right and one's complexion, I choose doing Halloween right. Arthur may not be wearing the Batman utility belt either. To be honest, I can easily imagine him making calls in street clothes, and, obviously, his call was short and perfunctory. To Arthur, this is just a cynical candy grab, and that sort of attitude reflects poorly on all us phone trick or treaters. I don't want to tell you your business, Mrs. Gorbowski, but I'm not at all sure that Arthur *deserves* any candy. That may leave you with a surplus. What you might want to do with it is entirely up to you.

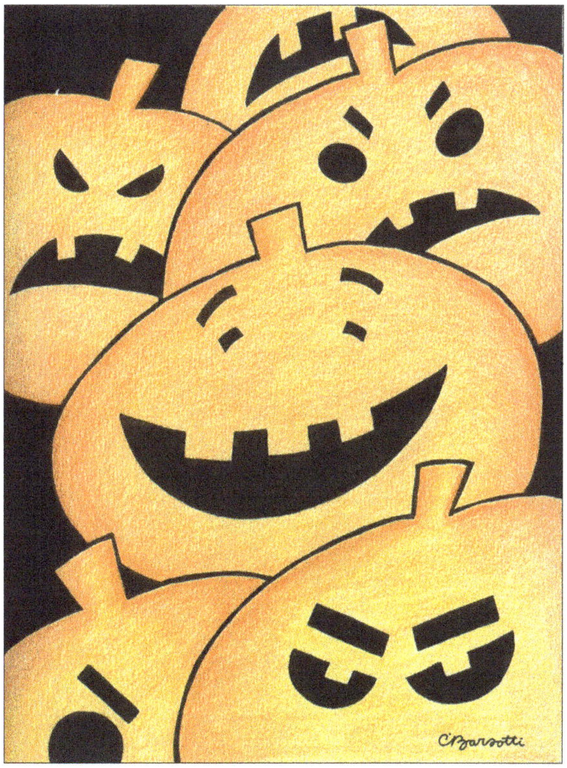
CBarsotti

Steve Young *(@pantssteve) is a veteran* **Letterman** *writer who's also written for* **The Simpsons**. *He's the main subject of the award-winning documentary,* **Bathtubs Over Broadway**.

Of course I'm really wearing a costume! I would never lie about that. I take Halloween very seriously. If you'd like, I can send you a notarized affidavit attesting to the fact that I wear my costume when I make my trick-or-treat calls. That would be an expense I'd have to pass on to you, of course. No, naturally you don't want to bother with that. You're making the right choice, Mrs. Gorbowski.

You've got someone at the door? Yes, I'll hold.

Hi! Welcome back! Or should I say, welcome boo! I said, "*Welcome boo!*" It's what a ghost might say. Again, I understand my high-quality ghost mask makes it a bit more difficult to hear me over the phone. Anyway, so was it an old school in-person trick-or-treater? Two? A vampire and a construction worker…hmm. Again, just my opinion, but to my mind the effect is diminished when two trick-or-treaters arrive together wearing costumes that destroy each other's reality. A construction worker wouldn't be casually hanging out with a vampire, and vice versa. I hope you didn't reward that. Plus, your commercially sourced outdoor-use costumes have to have safety reflectors and flashing lights, which really diminish the impact. My costume has a totally authentic, spooky look, untainted by any safety equipment or off-message association with a superhero or princess or what have you. I hope you'll agree, Mrs. Gorbowski, that my carefully curated presentation merits a generous allotment of candy. That name and address again is Ted Lewis, 19 Alder Lane.

Well, I should probably let you go. I'm sure you'll be fielding more calls and maybe even a live trick-or-treater or two. So just to quickly review, it's Ted Lewis, 19 Alder Lane, ghost, very well-presented, excellent robot the year before, and I think we're looking at least a dozen pieces of candy. You'll get the candy out in the mail tomorrow? Good, because this is trick-or-treating, and I'd hate to have to resort to tricks. Oh, you know, like more phone calls. Lots more lengthy phone calls. Right. Smart move, Mrs. Gorbowski. Bye! **B**

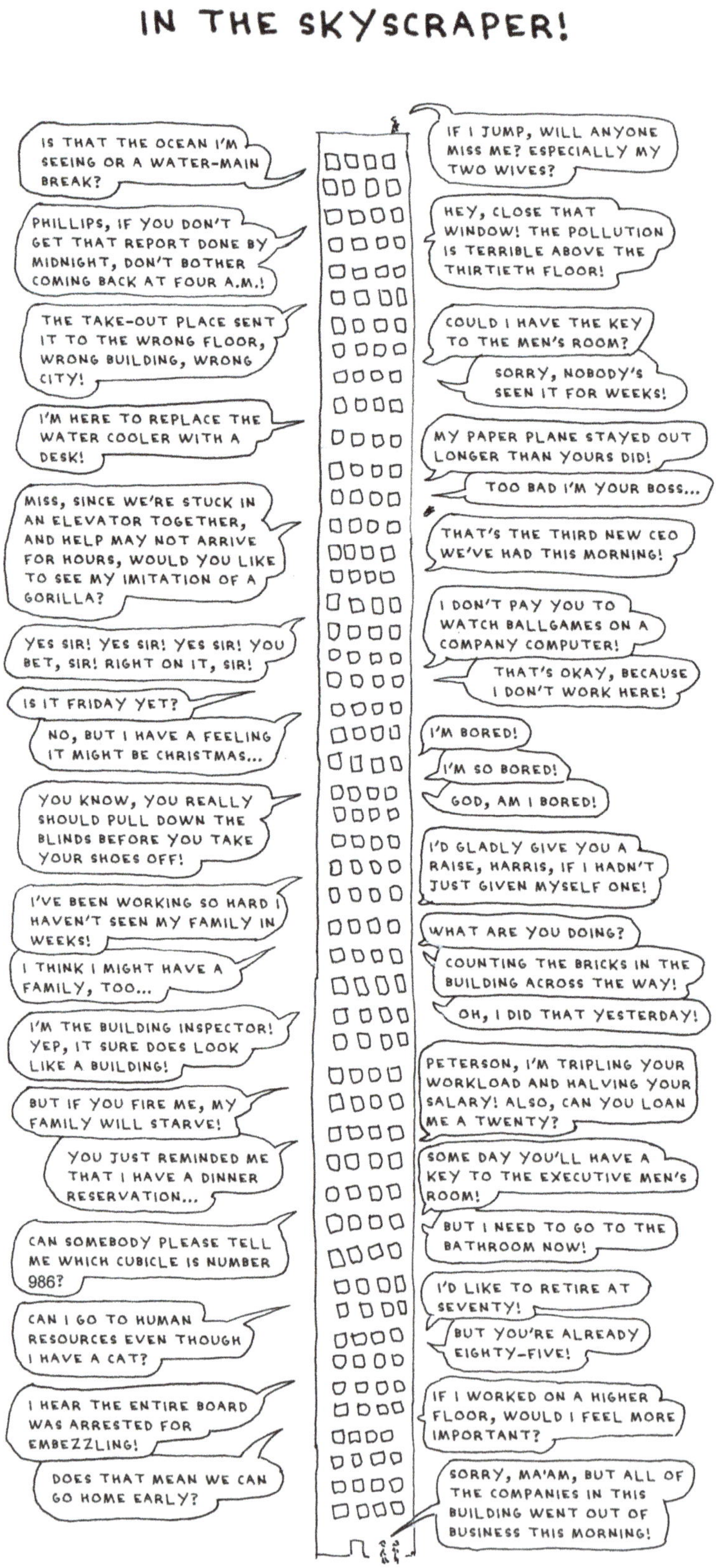
IN THE SKYSCRAPER!
IS THAT THE OCEAN I'M SEEING OR A WATER-MAIN BREAK?
PHILLIPS, IF YOU DON'T GET THAT REPORT DONE BY MIDNIGHT, DON'T BOTHER COMING BACK AT FOUR A.M.!
THE TAKE-OUT PLACE SENT IT TO THE WRONG FLOOR, WRONG BUILDING, WRONG CITY!
I'M HERE TO REPLACE THE WATER COOLER WITH A DESK!
MISS, SINCE WE'RE STUCK IN AN ELEVATOR TOGETHER, AND HELP MAY NOT ARRIVE FOR HOURS, WOULD YOU LIKE TO SEE MY IMITATION OF A GORILLA?
YES SIR! YES SIR! YES SIR! YOU BET, SIR! RIGHT ON IT, SIR!
IS IT FRIDAY YET?
NO, BUT I HAVE A FEELING IT MIGHT BE CHRISTMAS...
YOU KNOW, YOU REALLY SHOULD PULL DOWN THE BLINDS BEFORE YOU TAKE YOUR SHOES OFF!
I'VE BEEN WORKING SO HARD I HAVEN'T SEEN MY FAMILY IN WEEKS!
I THINK I MIGHT HAVE A FAMILY, TOO...
I'M THE BUILDING INSPECTOR! YEP, IT SURE DOES LOOK LIKE A BUILDING!
BUT IF YOU FIRE ME, MY FAMILY WILL STARVE!
YOU JUST REMINDED ME THAT I HAVE A DINNER RESERVATION...
CAN SOMEBODY PLEASE TELL ME WHICH CUBICLE IS NUMBER 986?
CAN I GO TO HUMAN RESOURCES EVEN THOUGH I HAVE A CAT?
I HEAR THE ENTIRE BOARD WAS ARRESTED FOR EMBEZZLING!
DOES THAT MEAN WE CAN GO HOME EARLY?
IF I JUMP, WILL ANYONE MISS ME? ESPECIALLY MY TWO WIVES?
HEY, CLOSE THAT WINDOW! THE POLLUTION IS TERRIBLE ABOVE THE THIRTIETH FLOOR!
COULD I HAVE THE KEY TO THE MEN'S ROOM?
SORRY, NOBODY'S SEEN IT FOR WEEKS!
MY PAPER PLANE STAYED OUT LONGER THAN YOURS DID!
TOO BAD I'M YOUR BOSS...
THAT'S THE THIRD NEW CEO WE'VE HAD THIS MORNING!
I DON'T PAY YOU TO WATCH BALLGAMES ON A COMPANY COMPUTER!
THAT'S OKAY, BECAUSE I DON'T WORK HERE!
I'M BORED!
I'M SO BORED!
GOD, AM I BORED!
I'D GLADLY GIVE YOU A RAISE, HARRIS, IF I HADN'T JUST GIVEN MYSELF ONE!
WHAT ARE YOU DOING?
COUNTING THE BRICKS IN THE BUILDING ACROSS THE WAY!
OH, I DID THAT YESTERDAY!
PETERSON, I'M TRIPLING YOUR WORKLOAD AND HALVING YOUR SALARY! ALSO, CAN YOU LOAN ME A TWENTY?
SOME DAY YOU'LL HAVE A KEY TO THE EXECUTIVE MEN'S ROOM!
BUT I NEED TO GO TO THE BATHROOM NOW!
I'D LIKE TO RETIRE AT SEVENTY!
BUT YOU'RE ALREADY EIGHTY-FIVE!
IF I WORKED ON A HIGHER FLOOR, WOULD I FEEL MORE IMPORTANT?
SORRY, MA'AM, BUT ALL OF THE COMPANIES IN THIS BUILDING WENT OUT OF BUSINESS THIS MORNING!

Ed Subitzky *was a Contributing Editor for* **The National Lampoon**. *His comics and humor writing appeared in nearly every issue.*

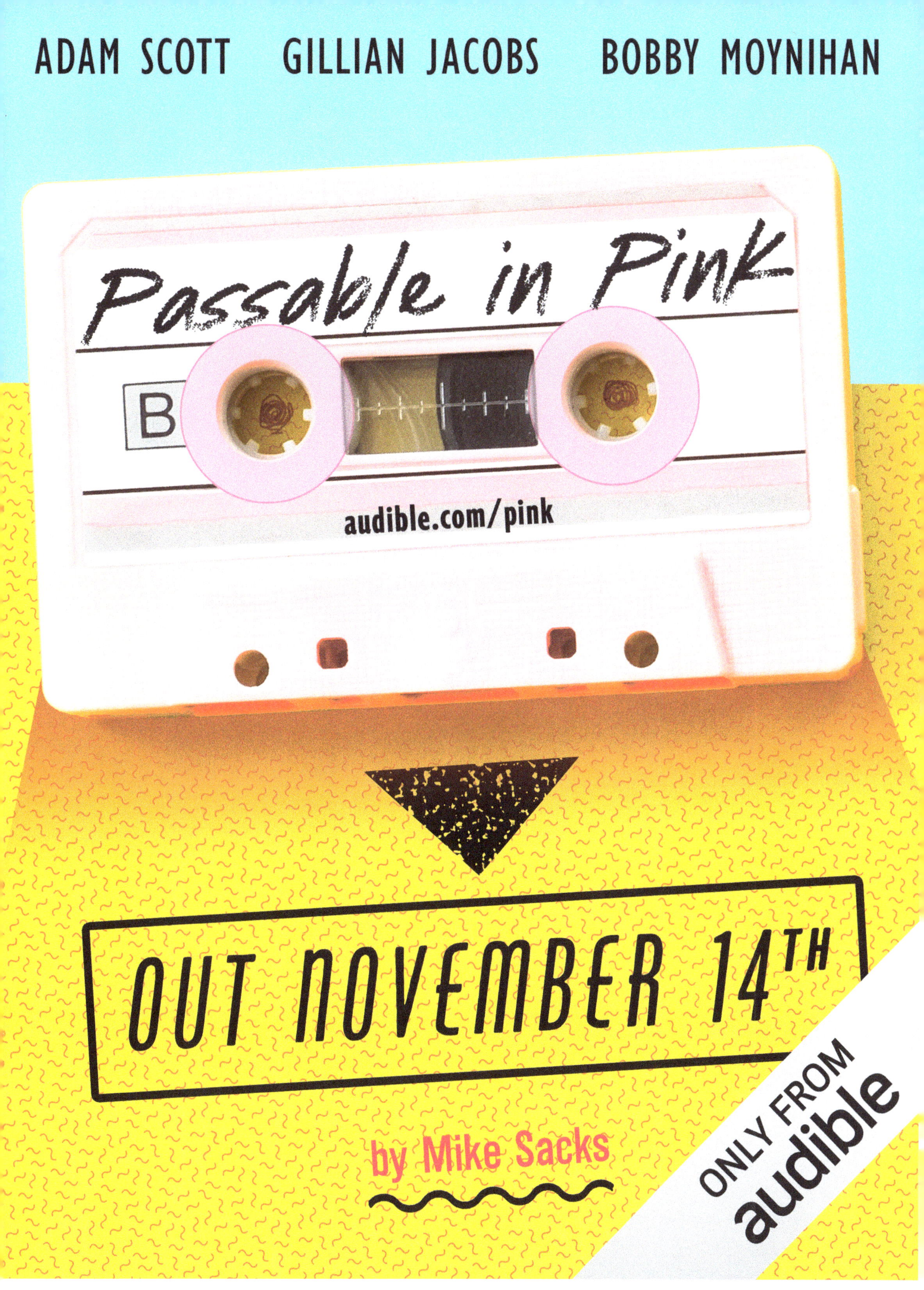
ADAM SCOTT GILLIAN JACOBS BOBBY MOYNIHAN
Passable in Pink
B
audible.com/pink
OUT NOVEMBER 14TH
by Mike Sacks
ONLY FROM
audible

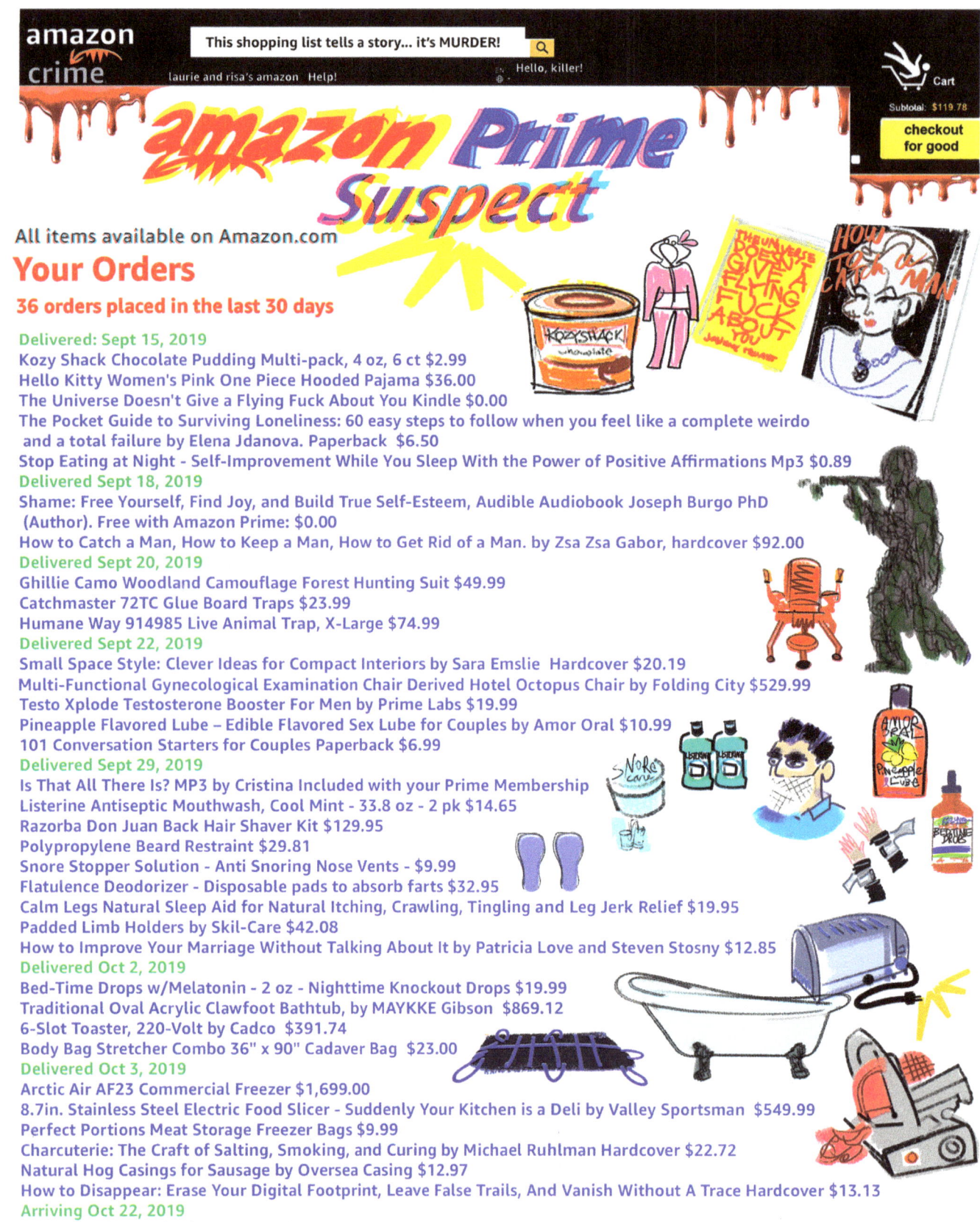

amazon
crime
This shopping list tells a story... it's MURDER!
laurie and risa's amazon Help!
Hello, killer!
Cart
Subtotal: $119.78
checkout for good
amazon Prime
Suspect

All items available on Amazon.com

KOZYSHACK
chocolate
THE UNIVERSE DOESN'T GIVE A FLYING FUCK ABOUT YOU
HOW TO CATCH A MAN

Your Orders

36 orders placed in the last 30 days

Delivered: Sept 15, 2019
Kozy Shack Chocolate Pudding Multi-pack, 4 oz, 6 ct $2.99
Hello Kitty Women's Pink One Piece Hooded Pajama $36.00
The Universe Doesn't Give a Flying Fuck About You Kindle $0.00
The Pocket Guide to Surviving Loneliness: 60 easy steps to follow when you feel like a complete weirdo and a total failure by Elena Jdanova. Paperback $6.50
Stop Eating at Night - Self-Improvement While You Sleep With the Power of Positive Affirmations Mp3 $0.89
Delivered Sept 18, 2019
Shame: Free Yourself, Find Joy, and Build True Self-Esteem, Audible Audiobook Joseph Burgo PhD (Author). Free with Amazon Prime: $0.00
How to Catch a Man, How to Keep a Man, How to Get Rid of a Man. by Zsa Zsa Gabor, hardcover $92.00
Delivered Sept 20, 2019
Ghillie Camo Woodland Camouflage Forest Hunting Suit $49.99
Catchmaster 72TC Glue Board Traps $23.99
Humane Way 914985 Live Animal Trap, X-Large $74.99
Delivered Sept 22, 2019
Small Space Style: Clever Ideas for Compact Interiors by Sara Emslie Hardcover $20.19
Multi-Functional Gynecological Examination Chair Derived Hotel Octopus Chair by Folding City $529.99
Testo Xplode Testosterone Booster For Men by Prime Labs $19.99
Pineapple Flavored Lube – Edible Flavored Sex Lube for Couples by Amor Oral $10.99
101 Conversation Starters for Couples Paperback $6.99

AMOR ORAL
Pineapple Lube

Delivered Sept 29, 2019
Is That All There Is? MP3 by Cristina Included with your Prime Membership
Listerine Antiseptic Mouthwash, Cool Mint - 33.8 oz - 2 pk $14.65
Razorba Don Juan Back Hair Shaver Kit $129.95
Polypropylene Beard Restraint $29.81
Snore Stopper Solution - Anti Snoring Nose Vents - $9.99
Flatulence Deodorizer - Disposable pads to absorb farts $32.95
Calm Legs Natural Sleep Aid for Natural Itching, Crawling, Tingling and Leg Jerk Relief $19.95
Padded Limb Holders by Skil-Care $42.08
How to Improve Your Marriage Without Talking About It by Patricia Love and Steven Stosny $12.85
Delivered Oct 2, 2019
Bed-Time Drops w/Melatonin - 2 oz - Nighttime Knockout Drops $19.99
Traditional Oval Acrylic Clawfoot Bathtub, by MAYKKE Gibson $869.12
6-Slot Toaster, 220-Volt by Cadco $391.74
Body Bag Stretcher Combo 36" x 90" Cadaver Bag $23.00

Delivered Oct 3, 2019
Arctic Air AF23 Commercial Freezer $1,699.00
8.7in. Stainless Steel Electric Food Slicer - Suddenly Your Kitchen is a Deli by Valley Sportsman $549.99
Perfect Portions Meat Storage Freezer Bags $9.99
Charcuterie: The Craft of Salting, Smoking, and Curing by Michael Ruhlman Hardcover $22.72
Natural Hog Casings for Sausage by Oversea Casing $12.97
How to Disappear: Erase Your Digital Footprint, Leave False Trails, And Vanish Without A Trace Hardcover $13.13
Arriving Oct 22, 2019
The Gifts of Imperfection: Let Go of Who You Think You're Supposed to Be and Embrace Who You Are by Brené Brown Paperback $8.97
Kozy Shack Chocolate Pudding, 22 Ounce. 6 per case. $2.99 x6 Reorder

Laurie Rosenwald's *(@rosenworld) dating profile is sensible_underpants.*
Risa Mickenberg *(@taxidriverwisdom) wuz here.*

Final Instructions

(Current revisions drafted by Rudolph W. J. Giuliani on August 27, 2018 [1,2] and orally amended on August 28[3] and 31[4,5,6] and continuously from September 1[7] to the early morning hours of September 4. Revisions resumed January 25, 2019[8] with amendments March 19[9] and 20[10], April 4[11] and 26[12], and September 18[13] and 30[14]. All additions to previous final instructions issued on November 6, 2016 are underlined; deletions are struck through.

To Friends and Haters:

This comprises the complete and exclusive final instructions of PRESIDENT DONALD JOHN TRUMP (hereafter "PRESIDENT TRUMP") to be executed faithfully in the event he ever dies. Failure to adhere to this decree, in whole or in part, will result in the largest lawsuit in history.

I. MEDICAL DIRECTIVES

A. In the unlikely event that he falls ill and is unable to administer his own medical care, PRESIDENT TRUMP wishes it known that under no circumstance should any method of resuscitating him or prolonging his life go untried, deploying all technologies now known or yet to be invented throughout the universe, including but not limited to the best Jewish doctors, cloning, lightning, voodoo, thoughts and prayers, whole head transplant (to a physically fit, not at all fat, sexually commanding male caucasian, aged 18 to 29, or to a female, subject to approval by PRESIDENT TRUMP), or transfer of consciousness to an iPad or other computerized device, providing it cannot be shut down or destroyed no matter what actions it takes.

   i. Should these efforts fail, and no pulse is detected on seven occasions, nor breath in a mirror, nor whatever else, the body of PRESIDENT TRUMP will be deposited in the Presidential Vault in the basement of Trump Tower, New York, and checked in three days for signs of Resurrection or Undead state.

   ii. The physicians, hospitals, medical device makers and shamans who failed and failed badly will be ~~sued accordingly~~ charged with treason.

II. CORPSE DIRECTIVES

If, ~~many~~ thirty-five years from now, PRESIDENT TRUMP is determined to be irrevocably dead:

A. His earthly remains will be harvested of all viable organs, ~~to be sold on the black market~~ to be sent to the Smithsonian Museum for an agreed-upon sum.

B. The brain of PRESIDENT TRUMP will be flash-frozen and stored in perpetuity at the Cryonics Institute in Clinton Township, Michigan, which PRESIDENT TRUMP won even though everybody said it was impossible.

   i. Under no circumstances will the Trump brain be handed over to the FBI.

C. The hands of PRESIDENT TRUMP will be donated to the Ripley's Believe It Or Not Museum in Times Square, Manhattan, NY, where they will be displayed in the front lobby in a case made of the finest convex glass.

D. ~~Unsold~~ Remaining organs will be preserved in the best gold reliquaries, should PRESIDENT TRUMP require them at a later date.

E. The earthly vessel of PRESIDENT TRUMP will be prepared as described in the *Egyptian Book of the Dead*, then given a full *lube* and tanning at Good Sunsations in Chinatown, including happy ending, or if this portion of Manhattan is underwater, then a professional tanning and stuffing by a top taxidermist.

F. The hair of the body of PRESIDENT TRUMP will be prepared according to schematics kept in a code word system server at the Jet Propulsion Laboratory in La Cañada, California.

G. At the last minute the head of PRESIDENT TRUMP will be swapped with the head of a great-looking goat. The original head will be preserved in exotic oils, to be found at the PRESIDENT's bedside, to provide a guide for reconstructive surgery to the host face of his frozen brain in future times.

(continued on p. 40)

NOTES:

[1] "As a Nation Mourns McCain, Trump is Conspicuously Absent"—*The New York Times*

[2] "Facing a growing public outcry, President Donald Trump ordered U.S. flags brought back down to half-staff Monday to honor Arizona Sen. John McCain—hours after they had been raised."—*USA Today*

[3] McCain Family releases details of memorial, to take place at the Washington National Cathedral. Tributes by Presidents Barack Obama George W. Bush, Sen. Joseph Lieberman, and Dr. Henry Kissinger. Pallbearers include: Vice President Joseph Biden; Mayor Michael Bloomberg; Secretary William Cohen; Sens. Gary Hart, Phil Gramm, Sheldon Whitehouse and Russ Feingold; Gov. Tom Ridge; Fred Smith, Founder, Chairman & President of FedEx; and the Oscar-winning Producer/Director/Writer/Actor Warren Beatty. All are described as a "friend."

[4] "Trump Sits Alone 'Sulking' as Washington Pays its Respects to John McCain"—*The Guardian*

[5] "Aretha Franklin's Funeral Fit for a Queen"—CNN Video

[6] From "Everything That Happened at Aretha Franklin's 8-hour Funeral" in *The Washington Post*: Stevie Wonder, Gladys Knight, Jennifer Holliday, Fantasia, Chaka Khan, Smokey Robinson, Ariana Grande, and Faith Hill sang. Isiah Thomas, Clive Davis, Tyler Perry, Cicely Tyson, the Revs. Jesse Jackson and Al Sharpton, and President Bill Clinton spoke. Also, "Georgetown University professor Michael Eric Dyson…condemned President Trump for disrespecting Franklin by claiming that she once worked "for" him. "You lugubrious leech, you doppelgänger of deceit and deviance, you lethal liar, you dimwitted dictator, you foolish fascist," Dyson said. "She ain't work *for* you. She worked *above* you. She worked *beyond* you!'"

[7] "During the memorial for the late Sen. John McCain, the current president tweeted and played golf."— *USA Today*

[8] "One Thai businessman was so enamoured with his golden retriever that he reportedly paid £10,000 to cover the cost of an event featuring 60 monks, 80 guests, a motorcade funeral procession, *(page 40)*

Plate 45: The Loathsome Swine

Odious Odious Ignoramus

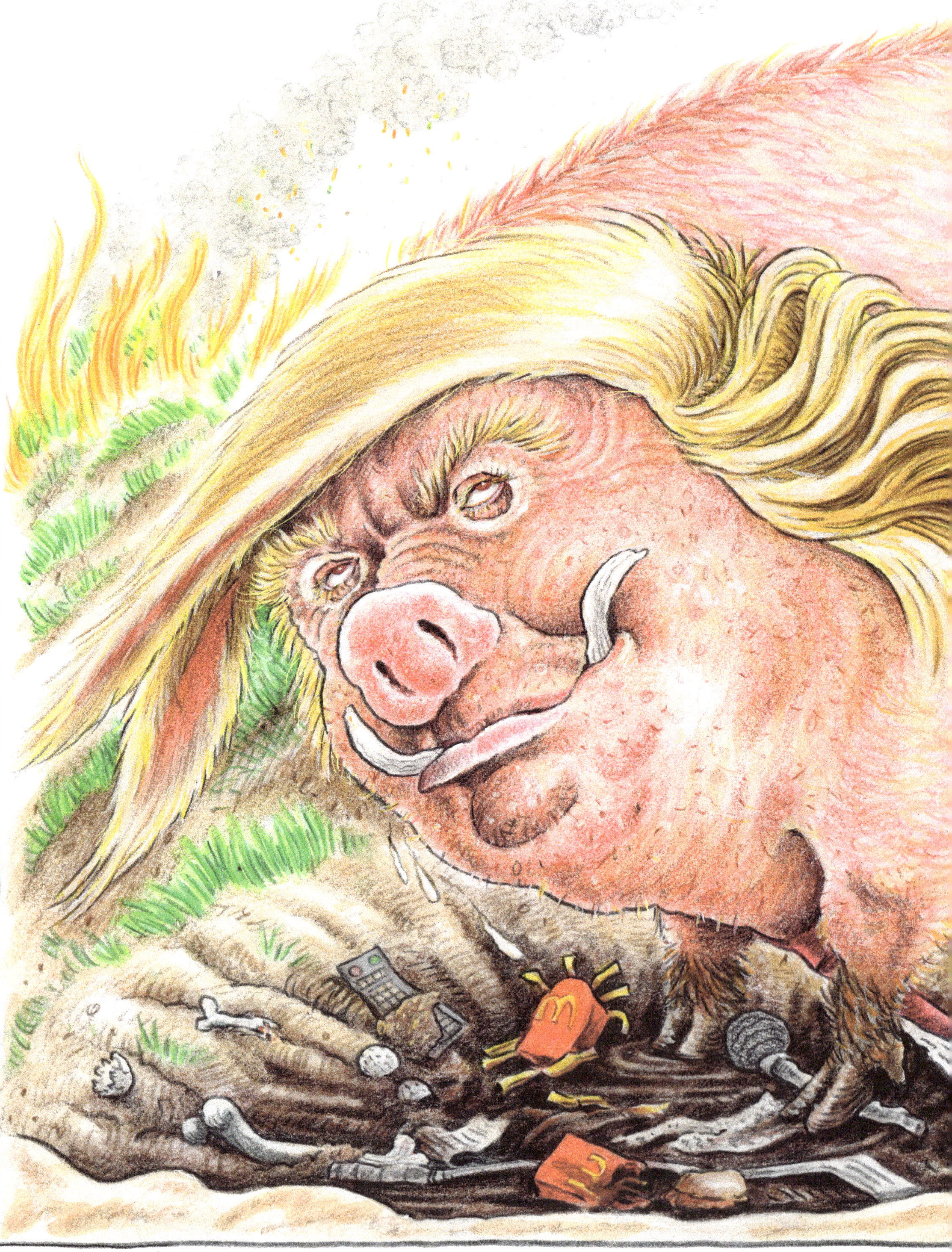

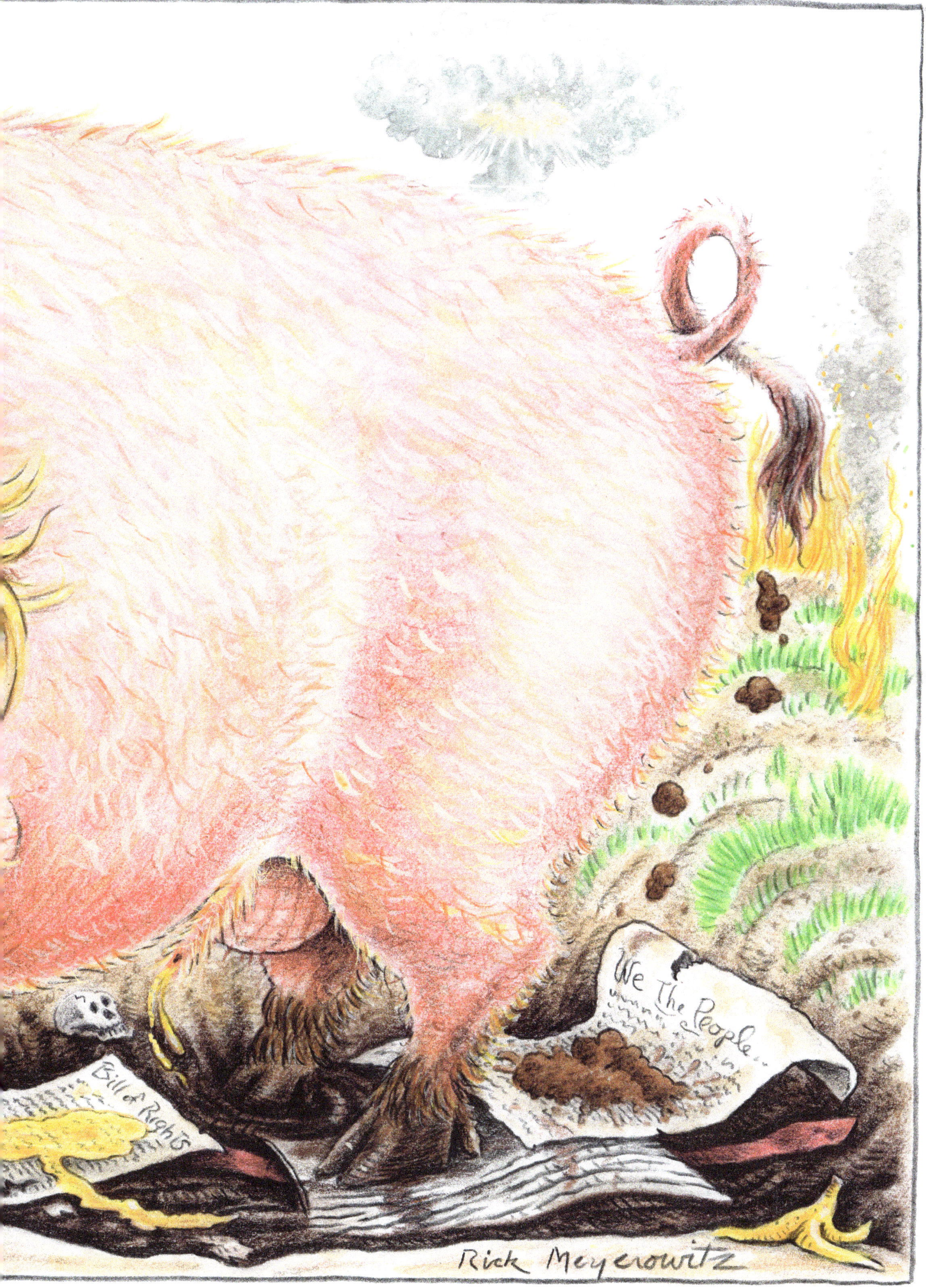
We The People...
Bill of Rights
Rick Meyerowitz

III VISITATION NOBODY HAS EVER SEEN BEFORE

A. P̲r̲e̲s̲i̲d̲e̲n̲t̲ Trump will lie in state in a couture backless Brioni suit, provided *pro bono*, for ~~three~~ twenty-eight days ~~at the Trump Grill in NY~~ in the Lincoln Memorial in Washington, D.C., in the lap of Honest Abe, who a lot of people don't know was a Republican.
  i. Or in a much larger Memorial constructed for the occasion.
  ii. So large.
B. Gold coins will be placed on his eyes, the likes of which Charon only dreams of, and Tanna leaves will be stuffed in all available pockets or fissures.
C. No less than twelve Banshees will be employed to provide 'round-the-clock wailing and vowing of revenge.
D. Flags of all nations and at Trump Properties worldwide will be kept at half-mast for ~~seven~~ one hundred days.
  i. During this period of mourning, gift shop and funeral concessions will be half-price, as will taxes on capital gains.

IV FUNERAL AND BEATIFICATION

A. P̲r̲e̲s̲i̲d̲e̲n̲t̲ Trump will be interred in a classy sarcophagus, equipped with compressed oxygen and state-of-the-art I've-Fallen-and-I-Can't-Get-Up technology.
B. The sarcophagus shall be carried ~~down Fifth Avenue, from Washington Square to Central Park, where it will circle three times before entering Trump Tower~~ by Adam Schiff, Nancy Pelosi, Hillary Clinton, Maggie Haberman, James Comey, Adam McCabe, Peter Strzok and his lover, the lovely Lisa Page — or if they are already dead or locked up, then by their children or grandchildren. The coffin will be greased and they will drop it, and out will spill assorted alligators and snakes, or if these prove too expensive, ten thousand spiders.
C. The real sarcophagus will be solid gold with pearl, onyx and diamonds, set in tableaus depicting P̲r̲e̲s̲i̲d̲e̲n̲t̲ Trump's Twelve Stations of Greatness (if more, then continued on the underside). It will be carried by contest winners to Arlington National Cemetery, to a five-square-acre plot that has been cleared for this purpose.
i. In addition to being made of the finest materials available anywhere, sarcophagus must be bullet- and firebomb-proof.
D. The sarcophagus will be placed in a modest gold pyramid atop ~~Trump Tower~~ the Washington Monument with a western exposure, casting an afternoon shadow on the Kennedys.
E. Several individuals (list attached) will be invited, and then disinvited from the ceremony.
F. There will be a 22-gun-salute, and then The Blue Angels will fly overhead. They will then fly overhead again, and again, until they run out of fuel and crash into the sea.
G. Eulogies will be provided by Abraham Lincoln, Ronald Reagan and Don King courtesy of Trumpmagic Animatrumponics from the President Donald J. Trump Presidential Library.
H. And Wonder Woman, who will tell mourners P̲r̲e̲s̲i̲d̲e̲n̲t̲ T̲r̲u̲m̲p̲ was "the best sex I ever had."
I. Elton John will sing a hit song written for the occasion, and not just new words on an old hit.
J. In a dramatic turn, Melanie Trump or a future wife will insist on being buried alive with her husband. Or failing that, a ten.
K. Pope Whoever Number Whatever will be on hand to acknowledge at least two miracles, including Greatest Economy Ever and avoiding untreatable venereal disease in the 80s.
L. US Space Force will provide security for the event, using super lasers to control the crowd in case of expected stampede or, if necessary, to provoke one.

V. FINANCIAL DISPOSITION

A. A sum of ~~one~~ five billion dollars ($15,000,000,000) in gold ingots and blood diamonds will be stashed in a below-ground hardened blast shelter, the location of which is known only to P̲r̲e̲s̲i̲d̲e̲n̲t̲ Trump's frozen brain or his encrypted iPad consciousness.
  i. Treasure and premises to be paid for by the Trump Organization via a loan from the Deutsche Bank or Russian Oligarchs, separately or in combination.
  ii. Silo will be attended by Eric Trump, wearing a royal purple tunic with gold brocade and Trump insignia. He will be sealed in with oxygen and provisions lasting 50 years, as well as three Real Doll™s of his choosing.
B. Donald Trump, Jr. will inherit the Trump Organization in its entirety, including all its debts, encumbrances, lawsuits and criminal liability.
C. Ivanka Trump, in thanks for her undying loyalty and continued hotness, will inherit the Trump brand, and the Presidency.
D. Any other children of P̲r̲e̲s̲i̲d̲e̲n̲t̲ Trump, if located and confirmed though DNA testing and ancient birthmark, will receive the sum of one-hundred dollars ($100), which is more than his father ever gave him.
E. P̲r̲e̲s̲i̲d̲e̲n̲t̲ Trump's likely ex-wife Melanie will inherit the Washington Monument. Maybe that will satisfy her. ₿

---

and an extravagant custom-built gold-plated coffin."—*Vice*
[9]"As he lay in an open casket at the Guido Funeral Home in Brooklyn, [Gallo's] sister Carmella vowed, 'The streets are going to run red with blood, Joey.'"—From "A Ranking of the Most Notable Mob Funerals in NYC History" in *The New York Post*
[10]"I gave him the kind of funeral that he wanted, which as president I had to approve," Trump vowed inaccurately. "I didn't get a thank you." — from *The Washington Post*
[11]"Thousands of devotees flocked to a mock palace of kaleidoscopic colours in Myanmar this week to dance, sing and pay their final respects at the lavish cremation of a local celebrity monk…Several storeys high and decked out in psychedelic colours and bright, flashing neon lights, the sacred building represented heaven.…For seven days, crowds flocked up the stairs of the makeshift palace to catch a glimpse of the abbot's body lying in an open casket, carried by a fluorescent dragon-shaped boat."—*Agence des Feuilles Politiques* (AFP)
[12]In attendance for Tony Stark's funeral were Spider-Man, Thor, Smart Hulk, Captain America, Dr. Strange, Black Panther, Hawkeye, Ant-Man, Wasp-Woman, Peter Quill, Rocket, Drax, Mantis, Nebula, and Groot.— from *Avengers: Endgame*. Oh, and SPOILER ALERT!
[13]Robert Mugabe, an authoritarian leader who ruled Zimbabwe for 37 years, "should be buried in a cave," said Benjamin Burombo Jr., a prominent traditional healer. When a Zvimba chief died, often his body would be dried, his teeth extracted and his finger and toenails ripped off. The body would then be wrapped in skin hides before burial, and could even be swapped with a token such as a goat's head to be buried instead.—From the ATP
[14]"Stalin's funeral led to a stampede in Moscow. Russians still remember the saying—'He lived bloody and he died bloody.' Eyewitnesses recall that lampposts and the sides of trucks used to block traffic in central Moscow were covered with blood."— From a review of "State Funeral," a found-footage documentary, in *The New Yorker*.

Back Issues

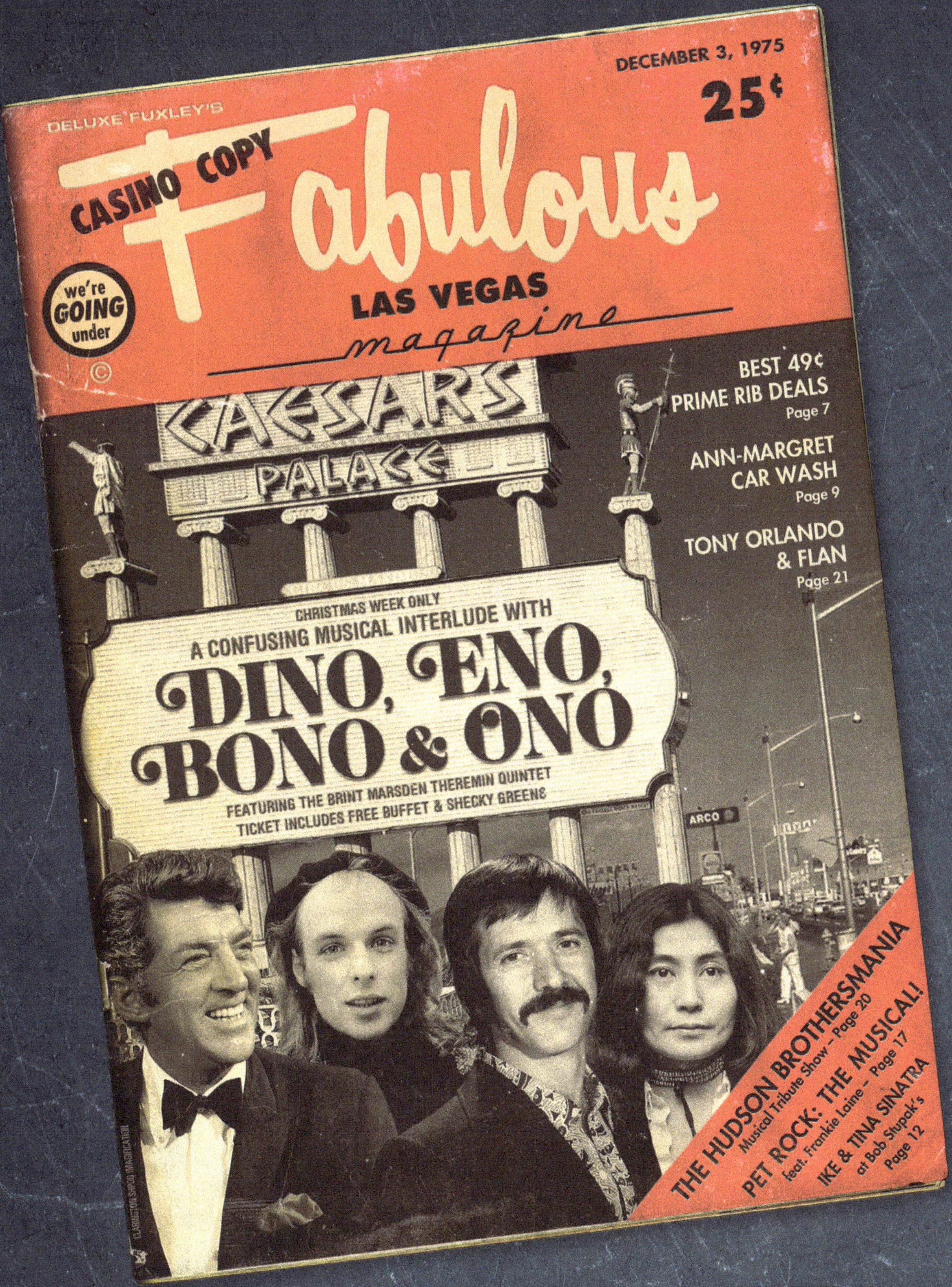
DECEMBER 3, 1975
25¢
DELUXE FUXLEY'S
CASINO COPY
Fabulous
LAS VEGAS
magazine
we're GOING under
©
CAESARS
PALACE
BEST 49¢
PRIME RIB DEALS
Page 7
ANN-MARGRET
CAR WASH
Page 9
TONY ORLANDO
& FLAN
Page 21
CHRISTMAS WEEK ONLY
A CONFUSING MUSICAL INTERLUDE WITH
DINO, ENO,
BONO & ONO
FEATURING THE BRINT MARSDEN THEREMIN QUINTET
TICKET INCLUDES FREE BUFFET & SHECKY GREENE
ARCO
THE HUDSON BROTHERSMANIA
Musical Tribute Show – Page 20
PET ROCK: THE MUSICAL!
feat. Frankie Laine – Page 17
IKE & TINA SINATRA
at Bob Stupak's
Page 12

Cris Shapan, *a Hollywood-based graphic designer and humorist, is more widely known by his "street name," Dirty CPAP.*

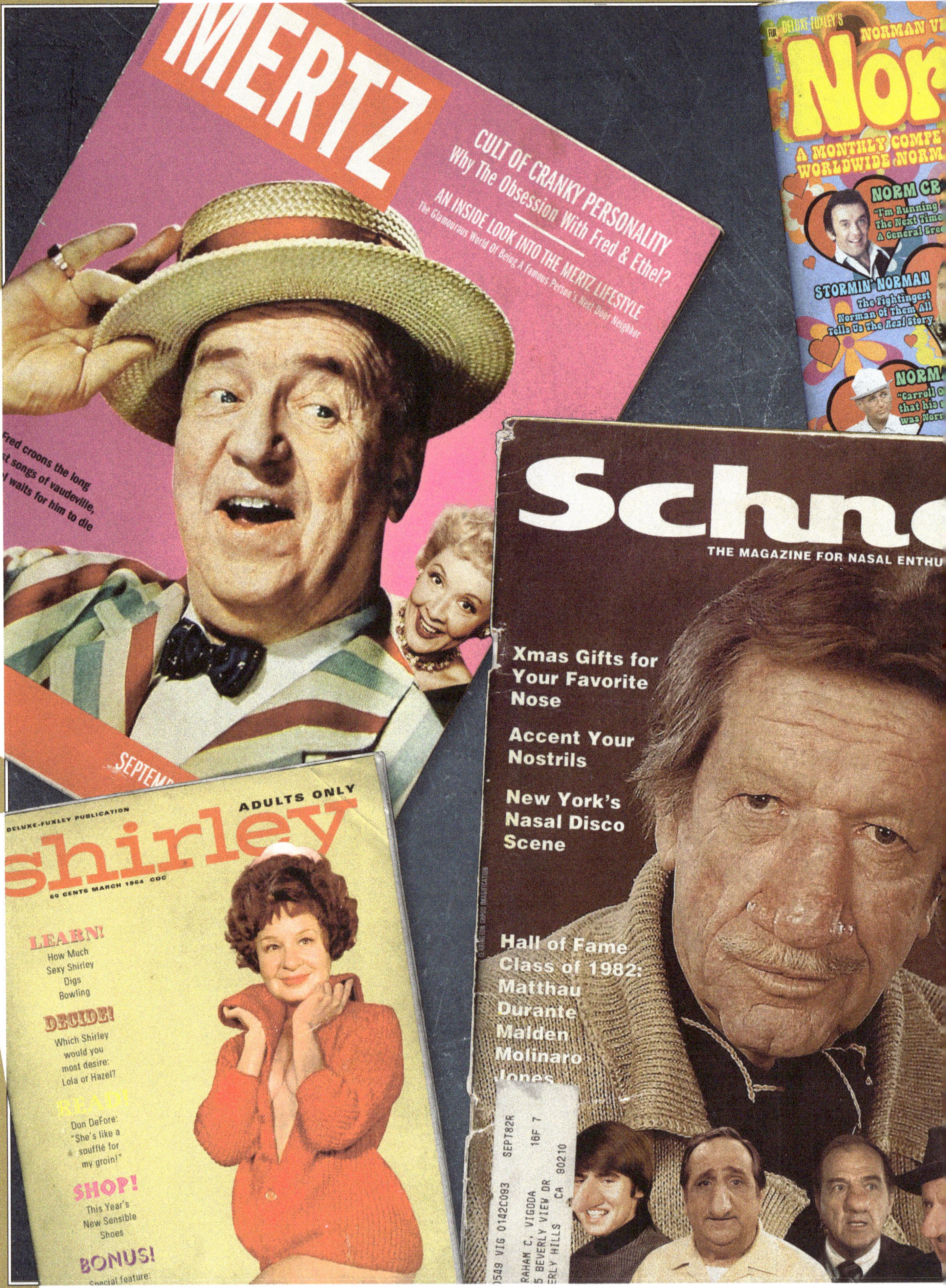
MERTZ
CULT OF CRANKY PERSONALITY
Why The Obsession With Fred & Ethel?
AN INSIDE LOOK INTO THE MERTZ LIFESTYLE
The Glamourous World Of Being A Famous Person's Next Door Neighbor
Fred croons the long
st songs of vaudeville,
waits for him to die
SEPTEM
DELUXE-FUXLEY'S
NORMAN VI
Nor
A MONTHLY COMPE
WORLDWIDE NORM
NORM CR
"I'm Running
The Next Time
A General Ele
STORMIN' NORMAN
The Fightingest
Norman Of Them All
Tells Us The Real Story
NORM
"Carroll O
that his
was Norm
Schn
THE MAGAZINE FOR NASAL ENTHU
Xmas Gifts for Your Favorite Nose
Accent Your Nostrils
New York's Nasal Disco Scene
Hall of Fame Class of 1982: Matthau Durante Malden Molinaro Jones
SEPT82R 16F 7
0549 VIG 0142C093
RAHAM C. VIGODA
5 BEVERLY VIEW DR
ERLY HILLS CA 90210
DELUXE-FUXLEY PUBLICATION
ADULTS ONLY
shirley
50 CENTS MARCH 1964 CDC
LEARN!
How Much Sexy Shirley Digs Bowling
DECIDE!
Which Shirley would you most desire: Lola or Hazel?
READ!
Don DeFore: "She's like a soufflé for my groin!"
SHOP!
This Year's New Sensible Shoes
BONUS!
Special feature:

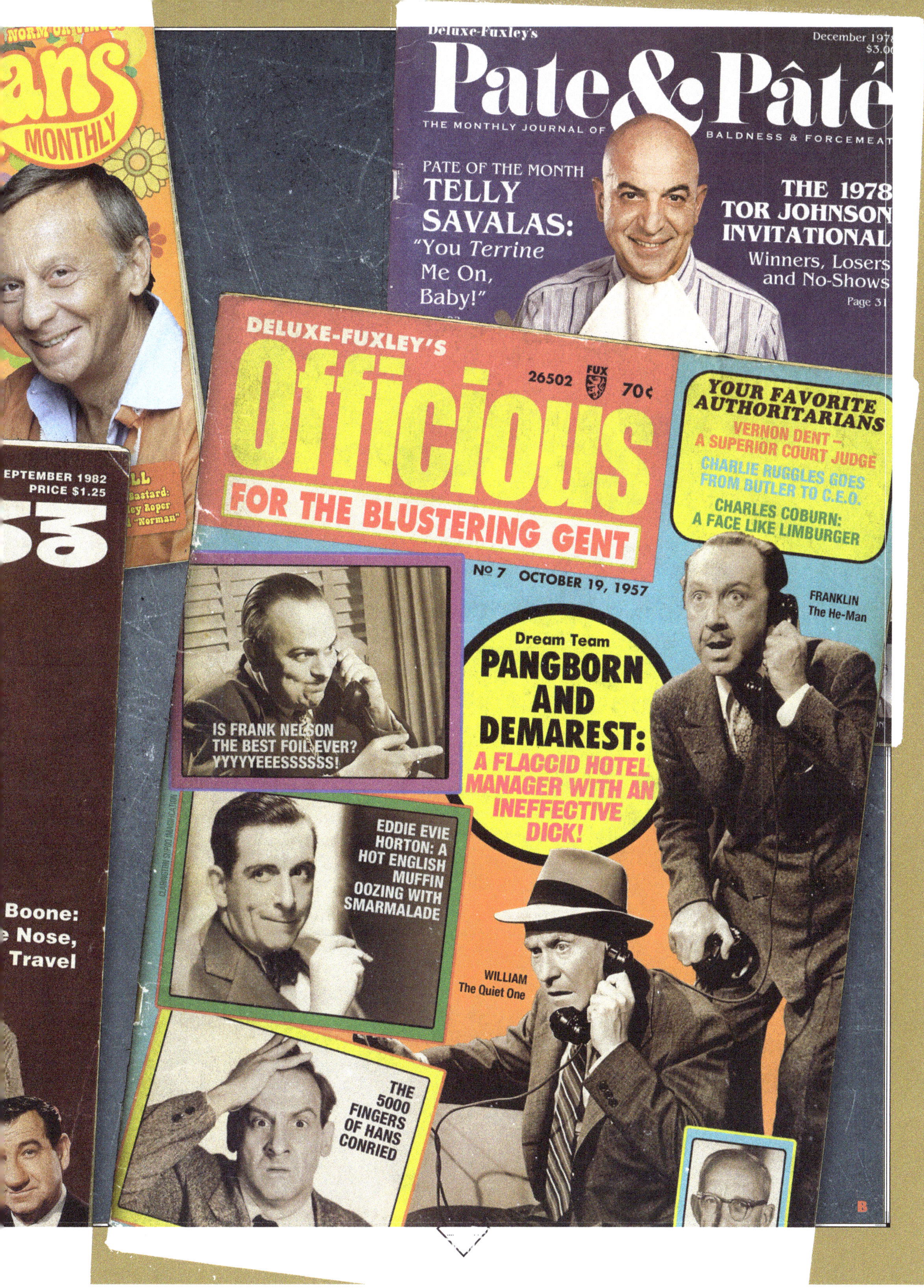

MONTHLY
Deluxe-Fuxley's
December 1978
Pate & Pâté
THE MONTHLY JOURNAL OF BALDNESS & FORCEMEAT
PATE OF THE MONTH
TELLY SAVALAS:
"You Terrine Me On, Baby!"
THE 1978 TOR JOHNSON INVITATIONAL
Winners, Losers and No-Shows
DELUXE-FUXLEY'S
Officious
26502
FUX
70¢
FOR THE BLUSTERING GENT
YOUR FAVORITE AUTHORITARIANS
VERNON DENT – A SUPERIOR COURT JUDGE
CHARLIE RUGGLES GOES FROM BUTLER TO C.E.O.
CHARLES COBURN: A FACE LIKE LIMBURGER
Nº 7 OCTOBER 19, 1957
FRANKLIN
The He-Man
Dream Team
PANGBORN AND DEMAREST:
A FLACCID HOTEL MANAGER WITH AN INEFFECTIVE DICK!
IS FRANK NELSON THE BEST FOIL EVER? YYYYYEEESSSSSS!
EDDIE EVIE HORTON: A HOT ENGLISH MUFFIN OOZING WITH SMARMALADE
WILLIAM
The Quiet One
THE 5000 FINGERS OF HANS CONRIED
EPTEMBER 1982
PRICE $1.25
Boone:
Nose,
Travel

FROM THE CAMPAIGN TRAIL OR THEREABOUTS

A New Satire Novel by Michael Bleicher & Andy Newton

"I almost died laughing. In fact, I probably should be dead."
—Richard Lewis
(Recovering comedian)

Weekly Humorist — The Standard in American Immaturity

HUMORISTBOOKS.COM

I Saw Milton Berle's Schlong

For those of you who don't know, Milton Berle (a.k.a. "Uncle Miltie," a.k.a. "Mr. Television") was a famous comedian who enjoyed a reputation for having a gigantic cock. The rumor followed him for his entire career. Writer Alan Zweibel said he saw the monster backstage at *SNL*, laid out on Berle's dressing room table, and that Gilda Radner had actually walked in on them. In Miltie's autobiography, he talks about a boasty stranger at a steam bath coming up to him and his pal Jackie Gleason demanding that Miltie compare penises. "Go ahead Milton," Gleason said. "Just take out enough to win."

For those of you who don't know me (i.e. everyone), I am a recovering model and actress who played mostly bitches, sluts, and whores in the 80's. I'm proud to say I am the first person to utter the word "condom" in prime time, when my character attempted to deflower Jason Bateman in Valerie Harper's show *Valerie's Family*. Among my other classy, memorable roles, I played bitchy slutty whores in *Casual Sex*, *Dangerous Curves* and John Hughes' *She's Having a Baby*.

In that last one, I was Alec Baldwin's gutter-mouthed girlfriend and shot a somewhat acrobatic, genuinely naked sex scene with him. I remember almost nothing about it—other than how his musky coat of thick, black chest hair looked like a million 70's female porn stars shaved off their pubes and glued them to his trunk. This immortal moment in movie history was cut because Hughes told me he thought I was going to be famous and would hate him forever if he kept it in. Sorry, John! Should've kept it in.

MILTON BERLE, seminal TV & radio comedian. Not pictured: his ginormous unit.

Anyhoo, I hated acting and came to L.A. to be a writer and director, so that's what I did. I'm proudest of my film *Love & Sex* with Jon Favreau and Famke Janssen, so please see that one if you want to judge.

In 1989, I wrote my first script (on a typewriter) after reading Syd Field's book *Screenplay: The Foundations of Screenwriting*. The script was a comedy about my awful experiences as an actress, and was called *Mary Lynn Butner Goes to Hollywood*. I got it to a producer named Randy Turrow, who knew my then-boyfriend (and current best bud), the talented writer and director Adam Rifkin.

Randy didn't buy that script, but was impressed enough that he called with an intriguing proposition: if I could come up with a good enough idea that could incorporate fifty "beauty queens" on a cruise ship, I could write and then direct the movie on an actual cruise ship that would be carrying real live hot girls from New Orleans to Cancun. "It'll be a six-day shoot," Randy said, "The boat leaves this coming Thursday."

I asked him if he knew that it was Monday.

"Yeah. I need a feature-length script and an entire cast in

•

Valerie Breiman *is a screenwriter and director. Her film,* **Love & Sex***, premiered and sold at Sundance in 2001. She is currently working on an animated series for Disney.*

three days. Call me back in an hour with an idea," Randy said, then hung up.

It's important to know that this was the era of home video, when tons of super-low-budget movies were being made. And because I was 25 and had that weird thing called "self confidence," I wasn't phased in the least. "Okay!" I thought. "If I write 20 pages a day, I'll have a 60-page script. Then, I can cast comedians in it and they can add their comedy routines, which will stretch it long enough to be feature length. Mom's right: *I'm a genius!*"

I called Randy back with a can't-miss pitch: "So, a nebbishy cruise ship waiter named Shecky dreams of becoming the ship's comedian, but gets bullied by the Evil Comedian on board who already has the gig. In the meantime, General Manuel Noriega sends terrorists to the ship to kidnap a bunch of the hot girls in bikinis. Our hero foils Noriega, becomes the ship's comedian, and ends up with one of the babes. It's called, *The Unsinkable Shecky Moskowitz!*"

There was a long pause, then: "Yeah. I guess that's okay." I was hired. Some rich guy put up a few grand, and my directing career began.

That's when the nerves hit. On the verge of puking, I sat down at my giant 80s desktop computer to write an entire movie in three days. (The finished product would one day inspire reviews like: "Sitting through this movie is worse than putting your dick in a blender." But I'm getting ahead of myself.) Over the next 72 sleepless hours, I wrote all day; at night, Randy and I hit the comedy clubs to cast the comedians.

One young comedian killed at The Improv. The audience loved him; he was known for playing "Stud Boy" on MTV's *Remote Control*, a game show that I had never seen, but he had a sweet face and just the right amount of nebbish to play a guy named Shecky Moskowitz. (Which was a *huge* amount of nebbish.)

His name was Adam Sandler and he knew we were casting a movie, so he was a little nervous. When he came offstage, I told him he was hired and he was extremely excited. His skinny, blonde comedian buddy begged to play Shecky's best friend. I had already cast my pal Tom Hodges in that role, so I told David Spade "better luck next time."

The night before flying to New Orleans to catch the cruise, we brought our very excited, very naïve financier to the Improv to show him how this Stud Boy fella was going to make us all rich. That night, Sandler got up on stage bursting with confidence, did the exact same hilarious act, and, for whatever reason, *nobody laughed*. Our financier was...concerned.

"He's really, really funny," I said. "I swear! You gotta trust me!" Meanwhile, Adam apologized to me quietly. I told him "the audience sucked," while secretly wondering just how bad this movie was going to be for all of us.

Go figure, but the producer somehow managed to talk a lot of young dudes into going on a free cruise to Mexico filled with gorgeous women. Billy Zane played King Neptune, God of the Sea; actor/director Peter Berg was the manager of the ship's metal band "Yellow Teeth," in which the lead singer (Croaker) was played by the b.f. Adam Rifkin; lead guitarist and the animator of our opening credit sequence was future *Phineas & Ferb* creator Dan Povenmire; director Steve Brill played a sarcastic priest; Shecky's best friend Bob was brought to life by my friend Tom Hodges from TV's *The Hogan Family* and *Steel Magnolias*; and soap star Ricky Paull Goldin played one of the two cuddly (pre-9/11) terrorists.

We rounded out our cast with those who would be shooting on land when we got back: Burt Young of *Rocky* fame as General Noriega; my not-yet famous pal Billy Bob Thornton as an audience heckler; and, of course, Milton Berle and his schlong played themselves. ALL STAR CAST, BABY! But not *at the time*.

Because I had to actually shoot a long film on a short cruise, a lot of the making of the movie was a blur. But I will break down the experience into a few digestible moments so we can get to the point of this story, which is how I saw Uncle Miltie's infamously massive wiener.

The cast and crew landed in New Orleans and we caravanned to the harbor where everyone unloaded their suitcases. The ludicrously handsome Billy Zane, wearing an ascot and stylish fedora, brought two freezer-sized vintage steamer trunks from the 1930's as if he were (ironically) about to board the Titanic. To be fair, he brought his beautiful Australian wife along for the shoot, so one of the 800-ton trunks was actually hers. They changed their clothes about four times a day, so big luggage turned out to be a smart move. On the way to the dock, a flurry of chaos ensued when we learned the crew forgot the box of lenses. But they still had one lens, so we'll be fine!

It was only later that the Director of Photography admitted to me that he was going blind.

We were all led to our "ship." If you dipped a rusty Royal Caribbean ocean liner in a giant bucket of shit, you'd have the floating Greyhound bus we'd be calling home for the next six days.

Like the Navy patrol boat chugging up that Cambodian river in *Apocalypse Now*, copious amounts of alcohol and weed were consumed on our ship. Of course the patrol boat in *Apocalypse Now* didn't have 50 hot girls on it, including one who was engaged to be married yet kept whipping out her tit and sticking it in everyone's drinks. I won't name names, but let's just say pretty much everyone was fucking everyone. Consensually. Except for me. I was too nauseated from a combination of seasickness and paralyzing anxiety.

The shoot was pretty uneventful. We shot something like 15 pages a day, which, in movie terms, means no matter how shitty something was, it was perfect! We were shooting film

STAN MACK

back then, so the cameras were huge and film was expensive, so you got what you got.

As you can imagine, I learned a lot about the nuts and bolts of making a movie fast and cheap. I also learned the value of having a first A.D. because I did not have one.

The first A.D. does a lot. Most importantly, he or she is the one who screams at everyone to shut up and hit their positions so you can actually shoot the movie. Not having a first meant *I* was the one doing that.

Now, screaming and directing works great for men. But when you're a woman (in charge) screaming at a bunch of dudes, you are instantly put in the nagging, shrieky, "You're not the boss of me!" category and are either tuned out, or loathed like Hillary Clinton.

Being a female director, I have worked with a lot of guys, many (but not all!) of whom had a hard time being "told what to do." If you really want or *need* something from one of those types, you have to keep your tone non-threatening and suggest things, lest you become their mother. On a side note, being a female director totally helped my poker game. It taught me all the wily, wonderful, manipulative ways to separate angry men from their money. And, to bring us full circle back to our story, it also helped me to get one old-timey comedian to show me his mammoth kielbasa.

Back to the ship. It was flooded multiple times with raw sewage in the first couple of days, so pretty much everything smelled like poop for the entire cruise. On that boat, every deck was the poop deck. A lot of people barfed that week. I think Sandler might've been one of the barfers in the first few days of shooting.

The things that poor guy did without complaining! Mainly carrying that fifty-ton, two-dollar movie on his innocent little shoulders while wearing the world's dopiest sailor suit. He was, and still is, an incredibly nice guy and I am so grateful that somehow *The Unsinkable Shecky Moskowitz* didn't end his career before it began.

In spite of the fact that the movie is on every "worst movie ever made" list, it somehow did not destroy anyone's future careers. Quite the opposite: In addition to all the directors and stars-to-be, our P.A. Gabe Sachs went on to produce hugely successful TV shows like *Freaks & Geeks* and *Just Shoot Me*. Allen Covert, another P.A. on the ship, went on to produce and collaborate with Adam Sandler on nearly all of his films.

On the technical side of things, we shot the entire movie using the standard 4:3 TV aspect ratio instead of the aspect ratio for film. Translation: We shot a square movie for a rectangle screen so all the actors' heads were cut off when projected. At the "premiere," the projectionist had to remove the 1:85:1 gate so the audience could see who the bodies belonged to.

My editor, Rusty, was in his late eighties and we were all under the impression that he had edited tons of Jerry Lewis movies. This wasn't the case. He probably said something like he'd *seen* tons of Jerry Lewis movies. He edited our film using a Moviola. If you don't know what that is, please Google it because I can't describe it better than a photo. Sadly for me—and all of our future viewers—I didn't realize that I could actually tell the editor what to do. This added up to him leaving about 15 seconds of dead air after every joke. Rusty was adamant: "Ya gotta leave room for the *laugh*!"

Maybe that's a vaudeville thing.

Back on land, we shot a couple more days. Day one was Burt Young's scene playing General Noriega, and Adam Sandler's scene where Shecky is heckled by Billy Bob Thornton at The Laugh Factory. The Laugh Factory went without a hitch. A bunch of comedians were hanging around watching, including one nerdylooking guy named Jerry Seinfeld. Billy Bob was a friend of mine because I'd recently played the part of his psychotic wife in a one-man show he was doing. He said he'd be happy to play a little part in my "boat movie." It went very well and I thought, "Wow. Directing can almost be a little bit fun!"

STAN MACK

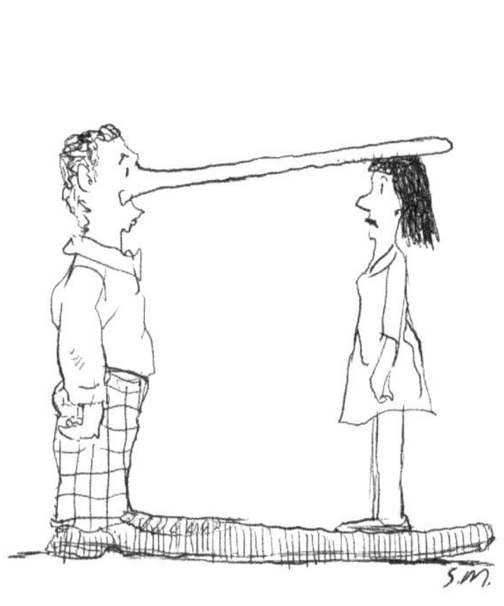
S.M.

Then I worked with Burt Young.

Burt only agreed to do the movie if he was supplied a jumbo-sized bottle of Jack Daniels to swig while working. It was clear he really, really, *really* didn't want to be there, but the Jack helped with that. (Until it didn't.) Young drank the whole thing over a two-hour period, and somehow managed to gurgle out some of his lines semi-coherently, while drenched in sweat and self-loathing. Conveniently, that all fit the character of Noriega perfectly. The trouble came when he started a series of irrational, spit-screaming tirades aimed at me, spewing, "YOU KEEP TELLING ME WHAT TO DOOOO, GODDAMN YOU! STOP FUCKING TELLING ME WHAT THE FUCK TO DO!!!"

In my newly adopted non-threatening tone, I gently reminded him that I was the director of the movie and that's actually my job. He told me to "FUCK THE FUCK OFF!" then passed out.

Day two was the big scene with Milton Berle. In the movie, Uncle Miltie is Shecky's idol and, in Shecky's fantasy, Miltie gives him advice on how to be funny while sitting at a table in an Italian restaurant. The location was some ancient place that smelled even older than it looked. It's long gone now and I can't even remember the name.

I was very excited to meet Milton Berle. Everyone was. We all got lots of pictures of ourselves with him and treated him like the God he was. Miltie showed up with a little card with all the jokes he wanted to tell written on it. We drew up huge cue cards for him and held them up behind Sandler.

It went very smoothly, even though none of us could understand the jokes he wrote for the scene. One of them was about a woman whose "tits were so small she had to carry her nipples in her

YOU ONLY NEED ONE 'YES'
101 ORIGINAL NEW CARTOONS

by Kaamran Hafeez

"An unbeatable combination—great jokes and great draftsmanship—a rare talent."
—Bob Mankoff

"This wonderful collection of classic cartoons you will revisit often is a tonic for all humans."
—Victoria Roberts

"This collection exemplifies draftsmanship and gagmanship and that's what single panel gag cartooning is all about."
—Matt Diffee

"God is unfair. He made Kaamran Hafeez able to draw better than me."
—Sam Gross

---

pocket." I haven't seen the movie since the 80s so I have no idea if that joke is in there. I do remember putting a laugh track after all his jokes (as an homage to his early days in television); and at the premiere he was so incensed by that he stormed out shouting, "I don't need a goddamn laugh track! This is bullshit!"

That was only 20 minutes after old-timey Vegas comedian Shecky Greene stormed out, shouting, "What a piece of crap!" (I was told later that Mr. Greene thought we were stealing his life story and went to the premiere to see if he had a case. But I digress.)

Throughout the day of the Berle shoot, between setups I kept hearing various male crewmembers talking about having just seen *it*. "Holy crap, it's huge." "The stories are totally true!" I probed a little, and found out that they were talking about spying Uncle Miltie's infamous monster dick!

I was instantly jealous. This was a once-in-a-lifetime opportunity! How could I live with myself if I missed it? I *had* to see Mr. Television's gargantuan joystick for myself. So I screwed up my courage, and asked him, very politely, if I could take a peek.

"No."

I was stunned. What the *fuck*? He'd shown it to the fucking second A.D.! I asked why, and he said he didn't want to show me because I'm a woman. This was 1989, pre #MeToo, so that was just balls-out misogyny!

I didn't give up. "Please?"

"No."

"Just a little of it, then? Maybe just the tip?"

"No."

"OK, what if I don't stare right at it?"

"NO."

We continued shooting. After the gaffer, an assistant cameraman and the craft service guy saw it, I asked one more time—and almost died when Berle said, "Fine, if it'll shut you up!" It was to be at the end of the day and my heart was filled with pure joy and anticipation.

After wrap, I looked around and spotted Miltie sitting in the back corner of the restaurant, sort of tucked away, talking to a crewmember. The crewmember left and I locked eyes with Berle. It was weird and awkward. I smiled and headed over; as I walked, my euphoria slowly turned to panic when I realized that, not only was I going to see *it*, I was going to have to react to *it*. Right in front of him.

My mind raced; I can't laugh. I can't scream. I can't spontaneously say, "Ewwwww!" or "Gross!" I can't grimace or shout, "Oh, my GOD!" What the hell am I gonna do?

I decided that the only appropriate reaction was to be calm, respectful and *incredibly* impressed, no matter what I saw come out of his pants.

When I arrived at his dark corner table, I tried a little small talk, but Berle clearly wanted to get right down to business. It felt weird, like I was a horny dude trying to make some poor tired hooker turn one more trick for half price after a long day. I decided eye contact was out of the question, so I acted all casual, looking around, waiting for him to get up and lead me to a discreet location.

He unbuckled his belt.

Wait a minute, he's not gonna stand up? He's just gonna open up right there on the—yep. The moment had arrived. I prepped my face for its calm and respectfully impressed expression, as he started to unzip the longest zipper I'd ever seen on pants.

Everything was sort of in slow motion from that point on. When the zipper hit the bottom, he opened the flaps of his slacks like a curtain.

And. There. IT. Was.

A giant, monstrous, purplish pile of cock, coiled on his lap like an obese, skinless cobra that was too fat and tired to strike. In other words, the rumors were true. I'm not sure how I would have felt at that moment had he just flopped it on the table, but I'm guessing it was even weirder seeing it nestled in his lap like a living, breathing, fleshy, twelve pound blobfish. I nodded with sincere reverence, calmly told him it was even bigger than I expected, and thanked him for his service. He stuffed it back in with a weary, "Yeah, I know" smile. Then *ziiiiip*, it was over. We said our goodbyes, and all three of us moved on with our lives—one of us changed forever.

And *that* is how I met Milton Berle and saw his mighty schnitzel.

May they rest in peace.

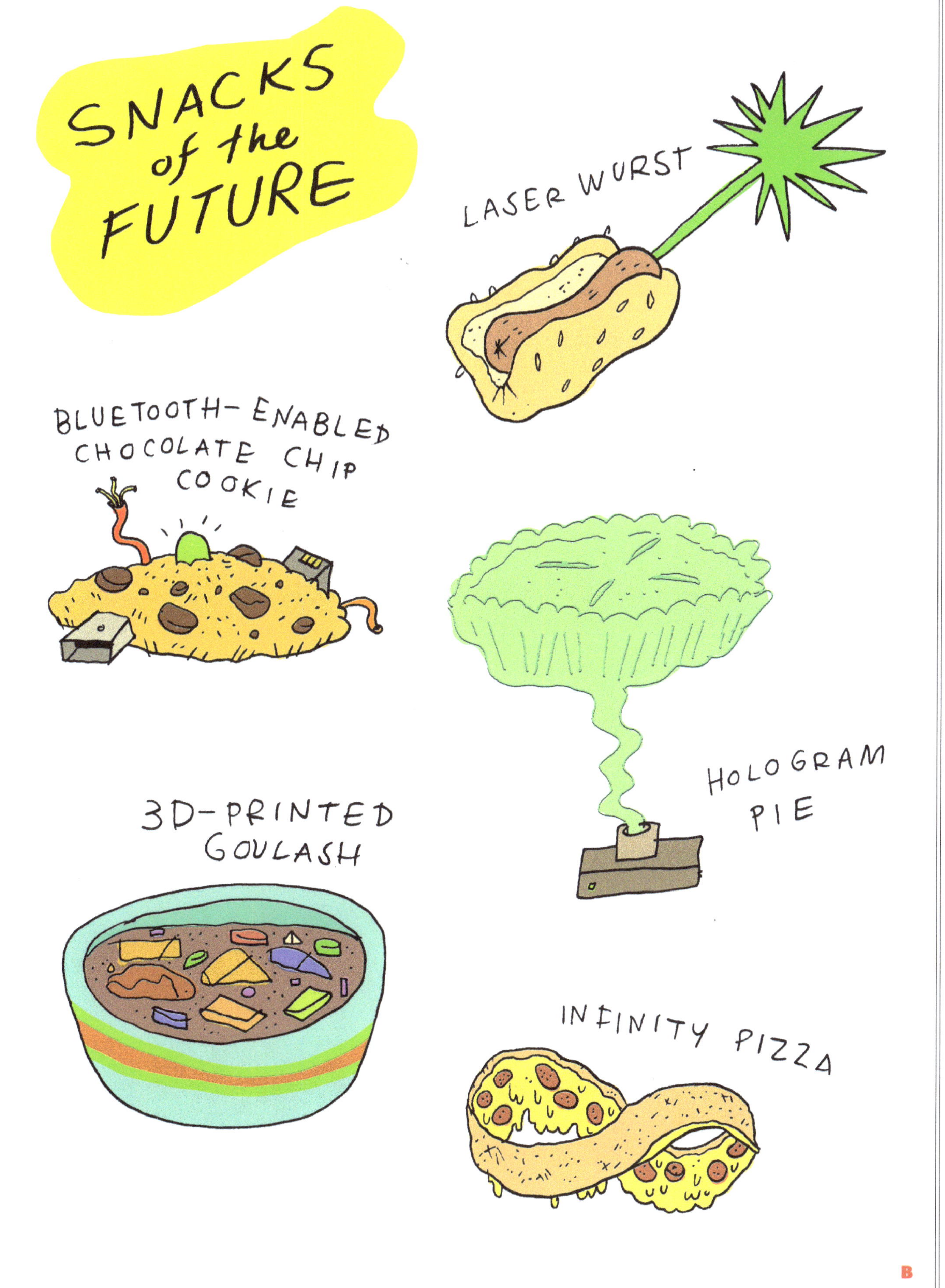
SNACKS of the FUTURE
LASER WURST
BLUETOOTH-ENABLED CHOCOLATE CHIP COOKIE
HOLOGRAM PIE
3D-PRINTED GOULASH
INFINITY PIZZA

A millennial couple faces the ultimate question: HOW TO LIVE AND LOVE IN AN AGE OF CATASTROPHE

—while managing the social media presence of the Old Testament God.

"With deep tenderness and a wonderful, feather-light sense of humor, Mr. Thier rehearses ancient conundrums over free will and the existence of evil."
—Sam Sacks, *Wall Street Journal*

"Captivating... Wonderfully zany."
—New York Times Book Review

"Thier is hilarious and provocative, his worldly insights sagely and frighteningly on the mark."
—*Booklist* (starred review)

Photo by Gesi Schilling

Aaron Thier is the author of the novels *Mr. Eternity*, a finalist for the Thurber Prize for American Humor, and *The Ghost Apple*, a semifinalist for the Thurber Prize. A contributor to the *Nation* and a graduate of Yale University and the MFA program at the University of Florida, Thier received a 2016 NEA Fellowship in Creative Writing.

BLOOMSBURY

Precautions for Flu Season

Autumn can be a stressful time. Not only are the days getting shorter, and the holidays are looming, but it's the beginning of flu season! Avoid the flu and have a safe, healthy, happy new year by taking these simple precautions.

1. Avoid close contact with sick people.

2. Wash your hands frequently with soap and warm water. If soap and warm water are unavailable, use an alcohol-based hand sanitizer.

3. If you have any reason to suspect a friend or acquaintance of illness, discontinue your social/romantic interaction immediately and give yourself a thorough "top to bottom" cleaning with antimicrobial soap, a non-polar solvent like acetone, and a disinfectant like bleach or lye.

4. Don't be fooled by the appearance of health. If you're considering having close contact (*i.e.*, a social/romantic interaction) with another person, whether that person is a stranger or someone of your acquaintance, ask that person if he or she is at risk of developing flu symptoms. If the answer is "yes," avoid close contact with them. If the answer is "no," scrutinize the shadows beneath their eyes. If you have any reason to imagine they're lying, avoid close contact with them.

5. But the truth is that it isn't safe to trust *anyone*, especially in flu season. Sick people are manipulative and self-interested, and healthy people may already be infected.

6. Tell everyone that you "just want to be left alone." Tell yourself the same thing.

7. Place a prominent mark or sign on your front door to warn friends, neighbors, acquaintances, solicitors, letter carriers, and other callers to stay away.

8. HARDEN YOUR HEART. If you're married or "in a relationship," insist on a trial separation. If your partner will not grant you a trial separation, terminate your marriage or relationship. (If you are unable or unwilling to terminate your marriage or relationship, skip to Precaution #36.)

9. Protect yourself whenever you have to appear in public.
    a. Wear Personal Protective Equipment (PPE). PPE includes lab coats or aprons, gloves, goggles, face masks, and shoe covers.
    b. Treat all strangers as you would treat a sick person (*i.e.*, avoid contact with them). Here are some tips for discouraging the affections of strangers:
        i. Wear a nun's habit (doubles as PPE).
        ii. Develop a significant facial tic.
        iii. Sing or hum tunelessly, at medium volume, while keeping your face as expressionless as possible. You may want to sing or hum such inoffensive songs as "Mary had a Little Lamb" or one of the themes from the Mario Bros. video games.
        iv. Perform the following dance step:
            1. Set your feet about a foot wider than shoulder width apart.
            2. Lean forward, keeping your back straight and your weight on the balls of your feet, and let your arms hang down in front of you so that the tips of your fingers are almost brushing the ground.
            3. Begin flexing and straightening your knees so that your posterior rises and falls rapidly.
            4. Keep your face as expressionless as possible.

10. When returning home from a public place, it's important to make sure you don't bring any germs inside with you. Take the following precautions:
    a. Convert your entryway or foyer into a hermetically sealed, germ-free chamber. This chamber should include, at a minimum:
        i. A laboratory shower.
        ii. An emergency eyewash station.
        iii. Double air-locks.
        iv. An autoclave in which clothes and other objects (*e.g.*, keys) can be sterilized.

Novelist **Aaron Thier** *was a Thurber Prize finalist for his book* **Mr. Eternity.** *His work has appeared in* **The Nation** *and* **Lucky Peach.**

"It wasn't me who called you a bitch. It was spell-check who called you a bitch."

v. An oven in which to perform dry-heat sterilization (an autoclave, which uses steam-heat, works more quickly but may damage some metals and cause powders to cake).
CAUTION: Be careful when removing objects from your autoclave or oven. These objects will be hot. Like all hot objects, they can cause painful burns. If you did not already know this about hot objects, please skip to Precaution #36.
b. After entering your germ-free entryway or foyer, immediately remove your clothing and place it in the autoclave for sterilization.
c. While your clothes are in the autoclave, take a laboratory shower and give yourself a vigorous cleaning with antimicrobial soap, a non-polar solvent like acetone, and a disinfectant like bleach or lye.

11. Don't leave your germ-free entryway or foyer.

12. Don't venture into the interior of your home except to use the bathroom. Follow these "bathroom safety" guidelines:
  a. Construct a sealed, sterile passageway between your bathroom and your germ-free entryway or foyer.
  b. Remove ALL your clothing before using the bathroom.
  c. After entering the bathroom, and again before leaving the bathroom, disinfect yourself with bleach or lye.
  d. DO NOT waste time considering the following: Sterilization destroys all life on the surface of, or contained within, the item to be sterilized. By this definition, it is IMPOSSIBLE to sterilize yourself, because you are a living organism. Disinfection, which simply reduces the number of targeted organisms to levels that the healthy body can tolerate, is the best you can hope for.
  e. After each use, sterilize the bathroom with one or all of the following reagents:
    i. Ozone
    CAUTION: Ozone is highly reactive and very hazardous to humans. It may also cause a bluish, gray, or purple discoloration of the skin.
    ii. Phthalaldehyde
    CAUTION: Phthalaldehyde causes severe irritation of mucous membranes and the upper respiratory tract. It may also cause a bluish, gray, or purple discoloration of the skin.
    iii. Ethylene Oxide
    CAUTION: Ethylene Oxide is explosive at concentrations greater than 3%. Exposure may cause irritation of the eyes and lungs, neurological damage, genetic damage, vomiting, and a bluish, gray, or purple discoloration of the skin. It is also a known human carcinogen.
    Hint: Sometimes you can avoid a trip to the bathroom by urinating in an empty container. Saving your urine is a good habit in any case because it's a way of preserving a record of your metabolic activity from one day to the next. If you're a girl/woman/female, try using a funnel.
    Hint: You may also want to save your "night soil" (i.e. feces). Use plain Tupperware containers and store in a chest freezer to prevent spoilage.

13. Food is one of the leading causes of contamination. Here are some helpful food safety guidelines:
  a. "Stock up" on the following foods well in advance of flu season. Try to restrict your diet to these foods.
    i. High-fructose corn syrup
    ii. Whey protein powder
    iii. Lemon juice
  b. If you have to make food purchases during flu season, do so online. NEVER visit a supermarket. Make sure to autoclave any food parcels you receive by mail.
  c. Before opening, place all food containers and packages in a vacuum chamber and mist with Hydrogen Peroxide vapor (30–35% concentration in aqueous solution).
  d. Before consumption, pass high-fructose corn syrup and lemon juice through a sterile filtration mechanism.
  e. Subject whey protein powder to dry-heat sterilization, or, since heat may affect the flavor, which is unpleasant enough to begin with, you can sterilize it with successive "impulsive loads" or shock waves.

14. Remember that protracted isola-

tion can lead to psychological problems like clinical depression, which compromises your immune system and makes you more susceptible to infection. While "hiding out" in your germ-free entryway or foyer:

a. Make sure to fill the lonely days with productive, rewarding, or amusing activities, which increase your chances of not succumbing to clinical depression and other disorders. For example:

i. Teach yourself to wiggle your ears.

ii. Maintain a hopeful outlook.

iii. Learn to play the flute!

CAUTION: Obtain your flute before flu season begins and sterilize it before and after each use.

b. Avoid feeling anxious. Persistent, high-level anxiety increases your chances of succumbing to clinical depression. If you begin to feel anxious, you may want to remind yourself that anxiety will almost certainly cause infection and everything (the elaborate, nightmarish, unspeakable pageant of illness) that comes with it.

c. Avoid communicating with human beings. Although the flu virus cannot be transmitted over the airwaves or through telephone wires, many people feel anxious when communicating (*i.e.*, talking, texting, chatting, sexting, skype-ing). By remaining out of touch, you also reduce your chances of getting bad news, saying the wrong thing, becoming exasperated, *etc.*, all of which could aggravate pre-existing feelings of desperation and lead to clinical depression. Remember that this doesn't mean you have to avoid communication altogether. Consider the following:

i. *Ouija Board:* It's a myth that two or more people are required for this activity. Plus, talking with the dead is absolutely safe. The dead are not at risk of developing flu symptoms.

ii. *Other Religions:* Talking to an image, totem, or idol is a great "safety valve," as is praying to the Judeo-Islamo-Christian God.

d. It's easy to become frustrated, especially in flu season. But remember that frustration can lead to poor decision-making and/or impulsive behavior, not to mention clinical depression. Avoid frustration.

e. If you believe that you're succumbing to clinical depression, put yourself on a regimen of antidepressant medication.

CAUTION: Doctor's offices, pharmacies, and hospitals are the MOST DANGEROUS places you can visit during flu season. DO NOT visit a doctor. Most antidepressants are available online without a prescription. Consult *www.easywebRX.com* for dosage hints and special discounts.

15. It's easy to get bored in a germ-free entryway or foyer, but try to make the best of it. Now is a great time to ponder the larger questions. For example:

a. If we were to encounter a species of compassionate and personable aliens, would they be offended by the representation of aliens in popular culture?

b. Across short distances, a cheetah is able to keep pace with a car moving at freeway speed. In the absence of other factors, an animal moving at this speed would experience winds of a corresponding velocity. Therefore, does it close its eyes when it runs?

16. Of course, questions beget questions. And if you find yourself thinking, perhaps with outrage, that even sick people are allowed to consume a range of food items and products not strictly limited to whey protein, lemon juice, and high-fructose corn syrup (to say nothing of the fact that sick people don't have to squat naked in a sealed chamber full of laboratory equipment; chatter away with ghosts, totems, and idols; and save their urine and/or night soil) consider the following:

a. Flu is not the real killer.

b. The real killer is the desperation caused by trying to avoid the flu, which will drive you (if you aren't careful) out into the world, into the society of people infected with every disease under the sun, and whip you to such a frenzy of ecstatic release that you might as well be a warm slab of agarose gel for all the good your immune system will do you.

c. In that sense, the sickness that kills is a sickness of the heart and the soul; a sickness of want or need.

d. The sickness that kills is the desire to love and be loved.

e. And THAT is what you have to avoid.

17. If you're still having doubts, just take the following quiz. Would you rather be:

a. A lonely flautist with a freezer full of night soil, or

b. Cold in your grave.

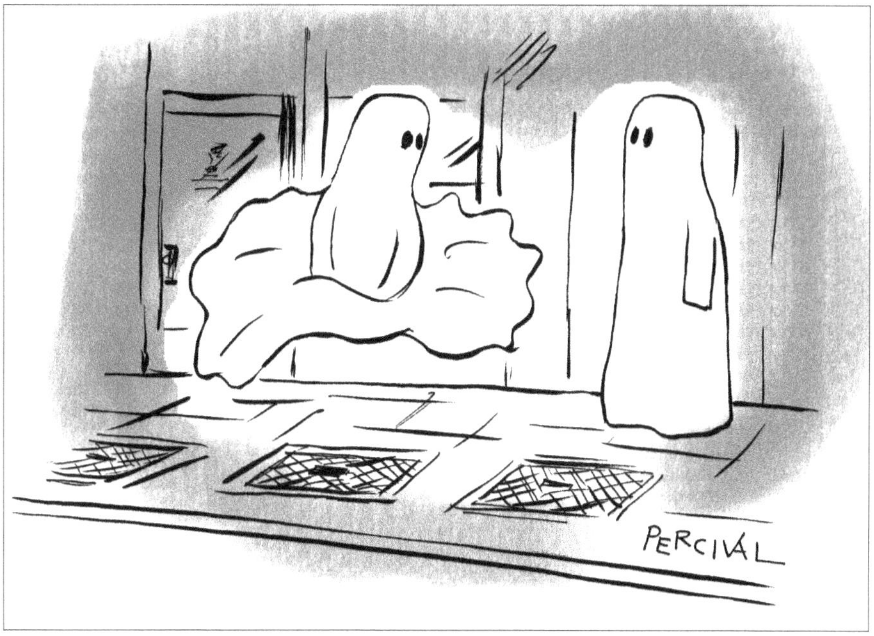
PERCIVAL

DON'T GO ON THE BEACH! By Brandon Hicks

ONE OF OUR FAVORITE SUMMER ACTIVITIES WAS PICKING UP SEA-GLASS ON THE SMALL STRIP OF BEACH IN FRONT OF OUR COTTAGE.
LOOK! PURPLE!
PLINK
THE GLASS CAME FROM DRUNK FISHERMEN TOSSING THEIR EMPTIES INTO THE BAY, OFTEN WHILE PISSING AND OCCAS-IONALLY FALLING OFF THE BOAT.
SPLASH
??
S.S. PEE
SOMETIMES, THESE FISHER-MEN WOULD GO MISSING AND WE'D HEAR ABOUT IT OVER THE RADIO.
...LAST NIGHT, AUTHORITIES SAY THAT WHILE THEY HAVE SENT OUT SEARCH PARTIES, THEY DO NOT FEEL OPTIMISTIC ABOUT...
THE EXPECTATION, THEN, WAS THAT THE BODY WOULD WASH UP ON OUR SHORE AT SOME POINT—NOT UNLIKE THE SEA GLASS.
THAT ALWAYS TOOK THE WIND OUT OF OUR BEACH HUNTS FOR THE REST OF THE MONTH...
...BUT IT WASN'T HALF AS BAD AS SWIMMING.
HEY! THE FISH ARE HITTING MY FEET!

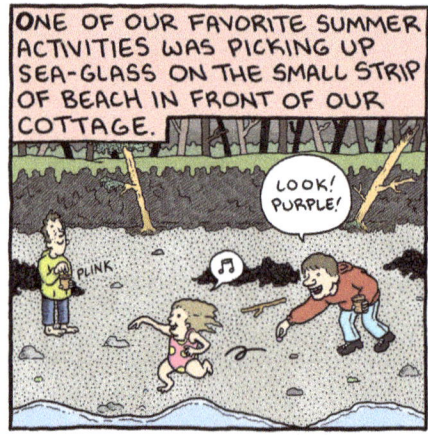

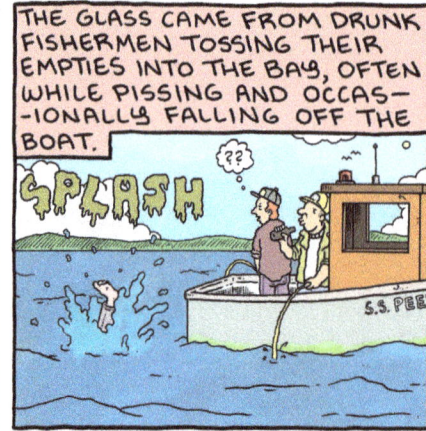

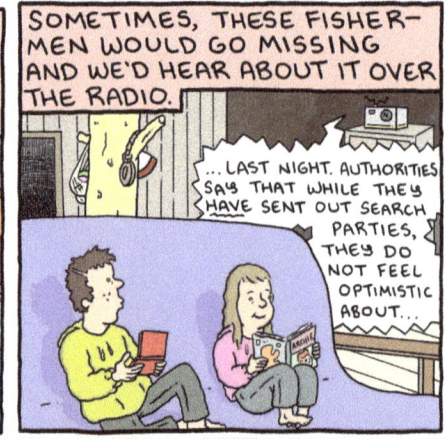

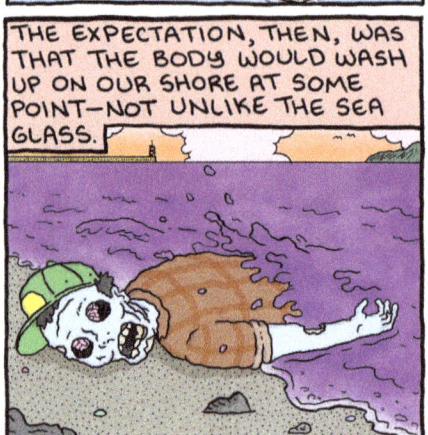

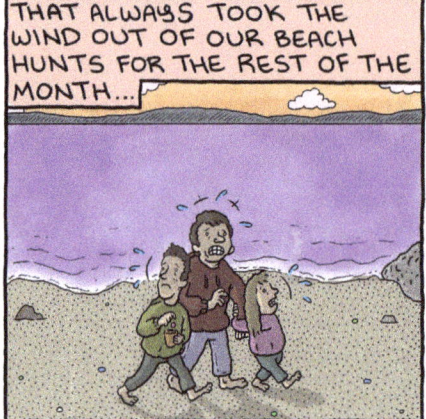

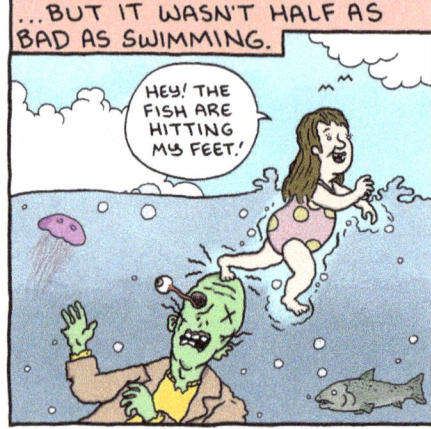

18. At the same time—My God!—who has the stomach for life, if this is what life is?

19. Or, to put it another way:
   a. What would you do differently if you knew that you had only a year to live?
   b. What if you had only one day?
   c. And what if you were to embrace the astonishing reality that you could die, flu or no flu, at any moment, any moment, any moment?
   d. Would you still be squatting naked beneath a scale replica of an Easter Island statue, breathing through a flute, your nostrils caked with protein powder, while your clothes cook in a homemade autoclave and you empty your bladder into an old lemon juice container?

20. Have a look in the mirror. Has your skin turned bluish, gray, or purple? Skin discoloration is probably the result of ozone, phthalaldehyde, and ethylene oxide exposure. On the other hand, it may be something else. It may be something even worse.

21. And is it possible that you didn't notice your skin was turning bluish, gray, or purple?

22. And is it possible that you didn't consider the feelings of your neighbors, alarmed as they must be by the toxic fumes and the persistent, noodling music of your flute?

23. And so, again, to repeat: Who has the stomach for life, if this is what life is?

24. There MAY be a big difference between clinical depression and the desperation induced by weeks or months of solitude, purification rituals, exposure to toxic chemicals, and regular commerce with the shadow-world of the dead. But who cares what it is?

25. Which is why you should place your canister of ethylene oxide next to the air-lock, rig up a fuse mechanism, and blow those fancy doors off their hinges. Then you should step through the smoke like an action hero and proceed into the winter night.

Hint: Protect yourself from the giant, toxic, extremely dangerous explosion.

26. Follow these guidelines when emerging from your home:
   a. Take deep, thirsty breaths of the cold fresh air, like someone saved from drowning.
   b. Remind yourself that interactions with your fellow humans can make life a joy.
   c. Remind yourself that a joyless life is not a life worth living.
   d. Remind yourself that no one lives forever.
   e. Remind yourself that night is only a shadow cast by the earth itself.
   f. Revel in this moment of voluptuous release, which is both a rising toward and a falling away; an affirmation of life and a renunciation of life.

27. Try to attend a noisy party in a small room. There are too many people there, it's hot like the inside of a human being, and the music is calamitously loud. You might even get lucky! And if

you succumb to an illness in a place like this, all that will be left of you is a pile of toxic ash glowing and pulsing by the bathroom door.

28. Locate a sick person and put your whole mouth on him or her. The best ones have eyes like blast craters and skin like the surface of the moon.

29. "Make out" with a dog. People say that a dog's mouth is actually cleaner than the mouth of a human being. To those people you might want to say, "How much cat shit did you eat today?"

30. Find out if your husband/wife or boyfriend/girlfriend will forgive you. Make all the apologies you need to make, with frequent references to your battle with, and subsequent deliverance from, clinical depression.

31. And then take a good look at yourself, with your tattered nun's habit dragging around your ankles and an expression of degenerate cunning on your face. Is this a person miraculously delivered from clinical depression?

32. Never mind, because now is the time to do all the things you've never done before, not even in the long-ago and brilliant days before flu season. Each person will have his or her own list of things, but consider the following examples/suggestions:

    a. Eat a favorite curry out of a bowler hat.
    b. Poor hot coffee in your lap and sue the coffee company.
    c. Do tons of drugs.
    d. Stop doing tons of drugs.

33. But after everything, you're left with only what you've had all the time, even when you were squatting naked in your germ-free entryway or foyer, and that is: Your own self. And a sense of isolation that pursues you wherever you go, whoever you're with. That is the lesson of flu season.

34. Or is it?

35. Concentrate on the wild chill in the air. The short days, the long nights. What remains of life is a fever dream. And the universe is a cough coughed by a madman.

36. If it seems awful, if it seems unbelievable, remember that this is life—this is the "human condition"—especially in flu season. **B**

KUPER

REACH INBOX HERO

PLAY THE EPIC EMAIL GAME

AdventureSnack.com

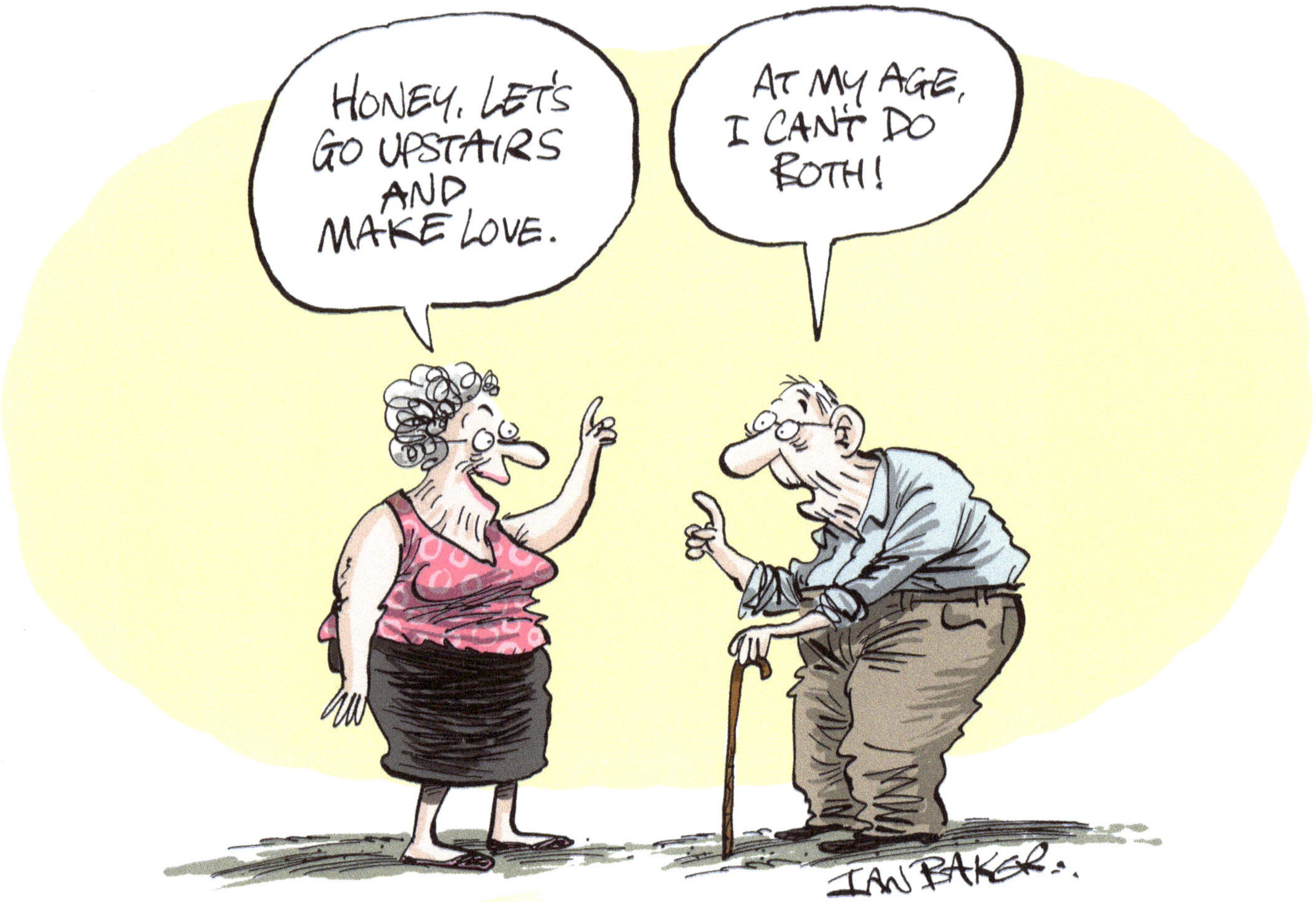
HONEY, LET'S GO UPSTAIRS AND MAKE LOVE.
AT MY AGE, I CAN'T DO BOTH!
IAN BAKER

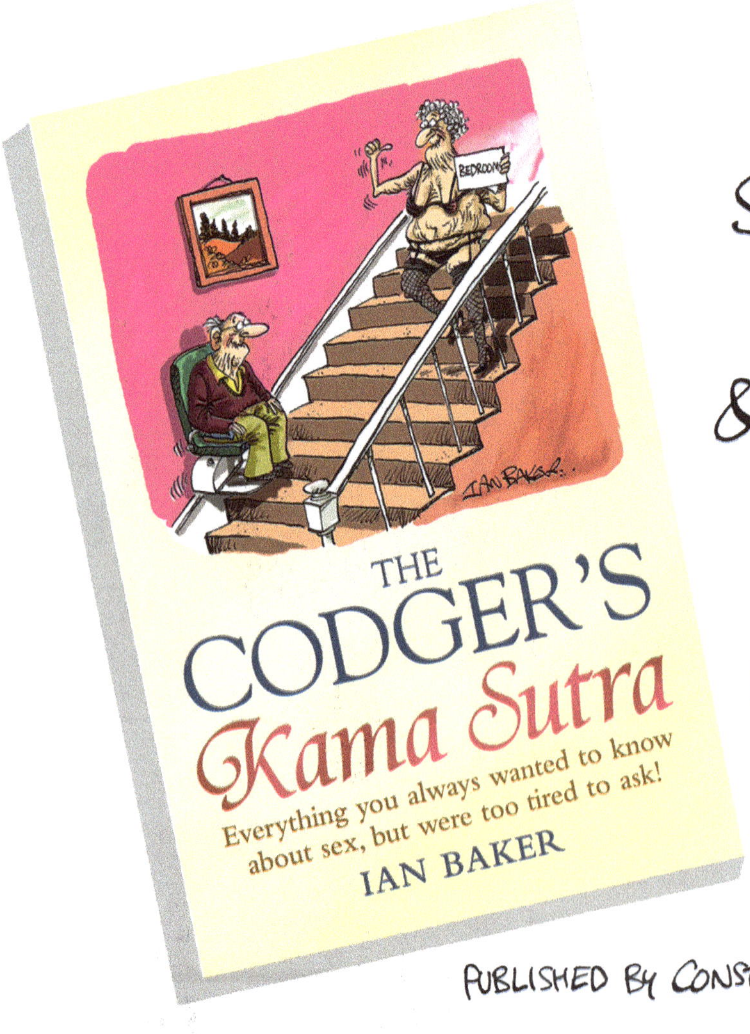
BEDROOM
IAN BAKER
THE CODGER'S
Kama Sutra
Everything you always wanted to know about sex, but were too tired to ask!
IAN BAKER

SOME CHRISTMAS STOCKING FILLERS HAVE CELLULITE & VARICOSE VEINS!

AVAILABLE FROM ALL DISREPUTABLE BOOKSHOPS AND AMAZON.COM

PUBLISHED BY CONSTABLE, AN IMPRINT OF LITTLE, BROWN.

I Was a Jewish Druid

DYLAN BRODY

I was raised culturally Jewish. For a time I was a practicing Druid. I'm a sporadically studying Taoist and I've recently developed a fascination with astrophysics, the Big Bang, and String Theory. I am a Jewish Zen Pagan with a newish yen for Sagan.

(Parenthetically, let me say that this all drives my father-in-law nuts. He is a Southern Baptist Evangelical minister who, two weeks before my wedding, sent my bride a letter advising her not to marry me because, according to him, she is going to heaven and we will not be able to spend eternity together. This didn't really bother me all that much because I was already fairly intimidated by the whole "'til death do us part" deal but the letter offended me significantly, nonetheless.

In retaliation, the night before the wedding, when we all went out for dinner, I spent the whole time bringing up Jesus stuff and deliberately getting it wrong. I told him I really admired Jesus for his immortality and his ability to turn into a bat when threatened. "No," he told me with a forced patience in his voice. "I believe you're thinking of Dracula."

"But there was something about drinking blood, right?" I said with a casual curiosity. I asked him what Jesus' superpowers were.

He said, "He fed the people on fishes and loaves."

"Really? Sandwich making? That's sort of a lame superpower."

"It wasn't a superpower, Dylan. It was a miracle!"

"Really? Sandwich making? I've done that miracle."

I took great pleasure in watching a vein throb in the forehead of this enraged man of god because I am not always a very good person.)

For my Druidic practices I had sanctified a small grove in a park near my home for ritual use.

It seemed to me one Halloween that I ought to do some sort of observance. So, I went to my little grove. I figured I'd get there around midnight and do a little thing, talk to the trees and say hi to some ancient Celtic Gods who rarely have anyone greet them these days.

I left my car in a space across the street from the park. As I was about to cross, a homeless guy approached me with a ghost mask pushed up onto the top of his head and a big bag of candy his hand. He held up the bag of candy, smiled and gave me a big thumbs-up. It occurred to me that Halloween is the one night of the year in this country when a homeless guy can feel like a participant instead of a pest. He was having a good night. I smiled and gave him a big thumbs-up.

I crossed the street toward my grove and became aware of the homeless guy crossing behind me. I was walking into a dark park late at night with a homeless guy right behind me. I quietly reminded myself that I was entering a sacred place, that nothing could hurt me here, that I was completely safe.

I entered my grove. The homeless guy sat down at the base of a big tree and began eating his sugary dinner. I moved from tree to tree, putting my hands against the bark and greeting them quietly. I thanked them for their beauty and their contribution to the atmosphere. I asked them for their guidance and their wisdom and their advice. They stood there and didn't say anything because they were trees.

As I stood with my hands against one of the trees, I became aware of five young Hispanic men moving toward me across the park. They were in their late teens or early twenties. They were drinking long-necked bottles of beer and speaking fast Spanish.

I began to get nervous. Demographically speaking, these are the people a middle-aged white guy like me is most supposed to fear late at night in a dark park. Deep shadows dominated the grove at ten minutes to midnight. I reminded myself that I was in my sacred space, that nothing could hurt me here, that I was completely safe.

The young Hispanic men stopped about seven feet away from me. I was invisible in the shadows. They did not know I was there. They spoke fast Spanish right next to me. I felt like a spy. I had no idea what they were saying because I don't speak Spanish, so I felt like a bad spy. Comprehension notwithstanding, I didn't want to be eavesdropping, so I stepped away from the tree and said, "Excuse me."

The young Hispanic men jumped and yelped, startled.

"I'm sorry. I didn't mean to scare you. I'm a Druid. I'm using this grove just now. Do you think you could come back in ten or fifteen minutes when I'm done?"

Dylan Brody is a playwright and humorist, poet and snappy dresser. Don't ask him about his tie. He'll talk for an hour about the Plattsburgh knot.

"Stan Mack shows that a man can be as caretaking as a woman, and a woman can be as brave, funny, and loving in death as in life. This compassionate, irresistible memoir is a gift to all of us."
Gloria Steinem, author, Moving Beyond Words

Janet & Me

An Illustrated Story of Love and Loss by
STAN MACK

Available now
at Amazon, Powell's or at your local booksellers.

Simon & Schuster

The six young men fanned out around me in a loose semi-circle. One of them assumed a position of leadership. He stepped forward just a little and said in a tone that may or may not have been intended as a threat, "Excuse me?"

At this moment I remembered the world's stupidest mugging, of which I had been a victim when I was twenty-one years old and living in New York.

I went up to Columbia University to hear my sister speak. Ronald Reagan was president, though he did not know it at the time. My sister was speaking about his Welfare Reform proposal, a horrible bit of ill-conceived budget-cutting based on the concept that the best way to discourage people from being poor is to take away their money. (This was before his successor decided the lynchpin of such reforms should be the Marriage Incentive, because nothing infuses a woman with a sense of independence and self-sufficiency like a state-mandated marriage of fiduciary convenience.)

My sister takes all of this very personally. I should explain: My sister is gay. I love her like a brother. She has a beautiful daughter who was deliberately conceived in a loving act between my sister and a turkey baster that was briefly filled with mail-ordered sperm. This, by the way, is one of the main reasons that I no longer do Thanksgiving dinner at my sister's house.

While my sister has certainly never been a slacker or a drain on society, she was briefly on government assistance after she was fired from her position as a bartender when the manager found out she had been breastfeeding her baby in a back room on a break. This occurred in an establishment, mind you, that proudly displays posters of the Coors Girls, because we live in this bizarre society where it's okay to use breasts to sell beer but not to feed children.

Leaving the lecture, I needed to take a bus back downtown. I walked off the collegiate safety of the Columbia University Campus and found myself waiting for a bus farther North on the island of Manhattan than any middle-class white guy has any right to be at eleven thirty at night. I sat on a bench in the January

◆

Halloween is the one night of the year when a homeless guy can feel like a participant instead of a pest.

◆

cold, blowing into my hands. My breath steamed in the night air.

A huge African-American man came and sat down next to me although it was the mid-eighties so at the time, he was still a big black guy. (For the record, this is not a reactionary anti-sensitivity joke about how everyone is too Politically Correct. This is a liberal, white, middle-class guilt joke about how I go out of my way not just to use the preferred language, but to use the preferred language appropriate to the period. I remember learning as a child that "midgets" preferred to be called "dwarves." I made the adjustment. Later I heard that the preferred nomenclature was "little people." Again, I adjusted, and if someday the choice is "person of small," I will adopt that language. Although, it's possible that some folks of limited stature might prefer other words entirely and are welcome to correct me. I certainly don't mean to imply that little people are a monolith.) The guy nodded at me. I nodded at him. We sat there with our breath steaming in the night air for a couple of minutes and then he said, "Give me all your money."

"What?"

"I'm mugging you. Give me all your money."

"Well...do you have a knife or something?"

He shrugged. "I could go inside and get a knife if you want."

I did not want that, so I gave him the six dollars I had in my pocket.

Then my mugger and I sat together on the bench, with our breath steaming in the night air. After about three minutes I realized there was a problem. "Well, now I can't get on the bus."

He said, "Oh. Sorry," and gave back a dollar, which was the cost of a bus ride in Manhattan in the mid-eighties.

I said, "Thank you," to my mugger and we sat there together waiting for the bus with our breath steaming in the night air.

The bus got there and I got on the empty late-night bus, aware of my mugger boarding right behind me. I thought maybe I should say something to the woman driving the bus, but at this point it was five dollars he'd taken so it seemed a lot less like reporting a crime than telling on a guy.

I paid my dollar and got on the bus. My mugger got on, paid a dollar and took a seat a few rows behind me.

We rode south together and after a couple of blocks my mugger tapped me on my shoulder. Startled, I jumped and yelped. I turned to see him holding out two dollars. "You know what? Why don't you take half this money back? You really always ought to have some cash on you."

That seemed sensible. I took the two dollars and again said "Thank you," to my mugger. He settled back into his seat.

We rode a few more blocks together and he rang the bell to signal the driver that he wanted to get off the bus. As the bus was coming to a stop he tapped me on the shoulder again. This time he was sheepish. He said, "You know, I really just needed bus fare. Why don't you take the rest of this back?" He offered me the last two dollars. We live in a bizarre society where it's less humiliating to be a criminal than a little short on cash.

By now I felt sort of like I'd bonded with my mugger, though. So I closed the money back into his hand. "You know what? Why don't you hold on to that? You really always ought to have some cash on you."

My mugger seemed a little surprised and said, "Thank you." He got off the bus.

The bus driver must have caught the end of this exchange in the rear view mirror and apparently she was a Reagan Republican because as we pulled away from the curb she looked at me in the reflection and said, "You know, you really shouldn't give them poor people money. It only encourages 'em."

All of this flashed across my mind as I was standing there, half-surrounded by these young Hispanic men in my grove with the moonlight filtering down through the trees. The leader said, "Excuse me? What did you just say to me?"

Before I could speak, the homeless guy stood up behind them. "He said..."

And the Hispanic men jumped and yelped and spun around, startled.

The homeless guy stepped out of the shadows. He said, "...we're Druids and we're using this grove. Could you come back in ten or fifteen minutes?"

The young men clustered a little tighter together and they spoke some very fast Spanish and then the leader said, "Yeah. Yeah. So...like, around twelve fifteen?"

"Yeah. That'd be great. Thanks."

They all started to move away together with their beers.

I threw the homeless guy a big thumbs-up and a smile. He smiled and threw me a thumbs-up happy to have been a participant rather than a pest. He sat down to finish his candy. I went back to the tree I had been greeting.

Right about this time one of the Hispanic boys turned back to look at the grove. I smiled and nodded but apparently I'd been swallowed up again by the tree's shadow because I heard him say, "Yo, Dudes! Where'd they go?" and as the others turned back to look toward the grove he said, "And how many do you think there were?" **B**

Give your kid a book just for laughs.

When James Patterson teams up with Joey Green, something funny happens.

Not So Normal Norbert is a rollicking adventure into a futuristic world, where different is dangerous, imagination is insanity, and creativity is crazy!

Norbert Riddle lives in the United State of Earth, where normal means following the rules, never standing out, and being exactly the same as everyone else, down to the plain gray jumpsuit he wears everyday. He's been normal his whole life—until a moment of temporary hilarity when he does a funny impression of their dictator, Loving Leader . . . and gets caught!

Now, Norbert's been arrested and banished to planet Zorquat 3 in the Orion Nebula, where kids who defy the rules roam free in the Astronuts camp. Norbert has been taught his whole life that different is wrong, but everyone at Astronuts is crazy, creative, and completely insane!

"Readers will chortle at the relentless wordplay, a supporting cast made up almost entirely of caricatured grown-ups and young pranksters, and Norbert's winning mix of glibness and gullibility."—*Booklist*

Funny books turn kids into serious readers.

Z*ggy Tuesdays

Cartoonist Paul Karasik found an old paperback in a flea market and bought it for a dollar. Every Tuesday, he posts his latest remix. Here are some of our favorites.

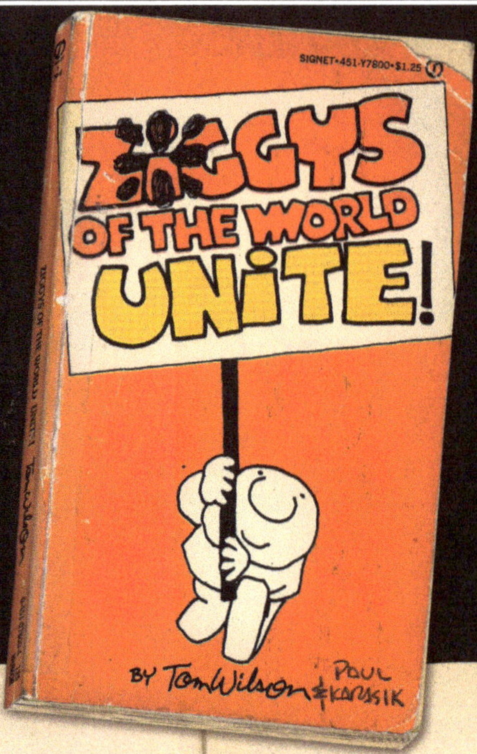
SIGNET•451-Y7800•$1.25
ZIGGYS
OF THE WORLD
UNITE!
BY Tom Wilson & PAUL KARASIK

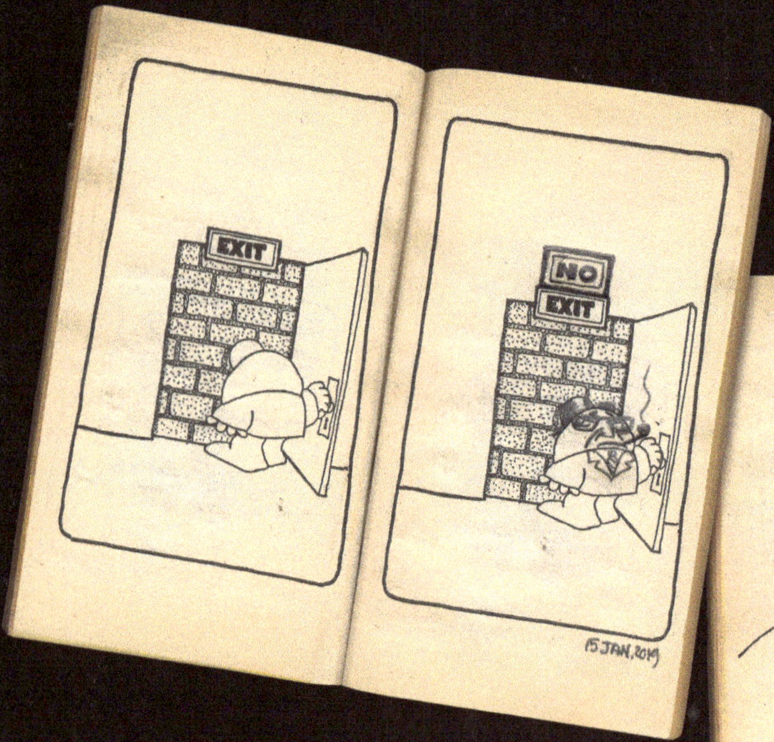
EXIT
NO
EXIT
15 JAN. 2019

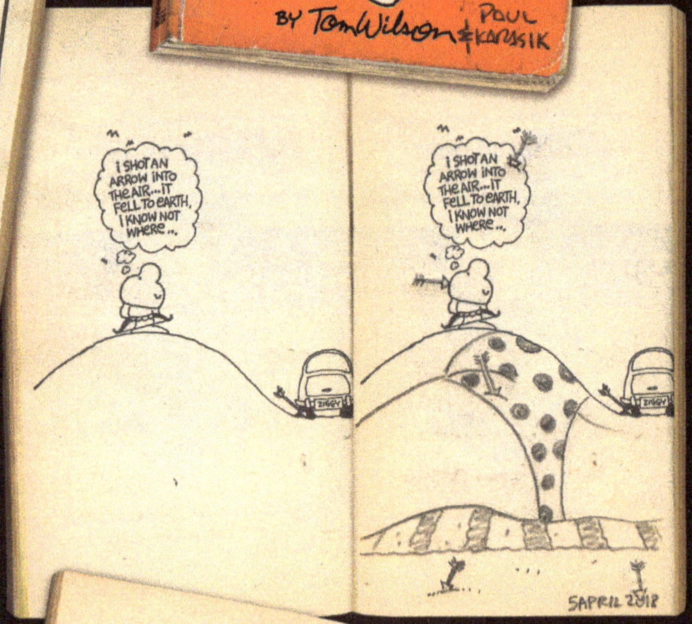
I SHOT AN ARROW INTO THE AIR... IT FELL TO EARTH, I KNOW NOT WHERE...
I SHOT AN ARROW INTO THE AIR... IT FELL TO EARTH, I KNOW NOT WHERE...
5 APRIL 2018

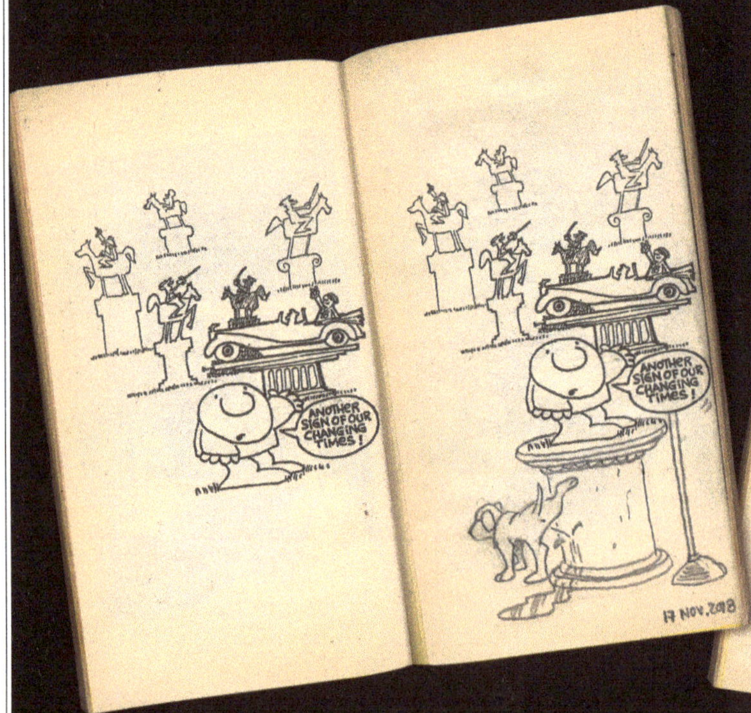
ANOTHER SIGN OF OUR CHANGING TIMES!
ANOTHER SIGN OF OUR CHANGING TIMES!
17 NOV. 2018

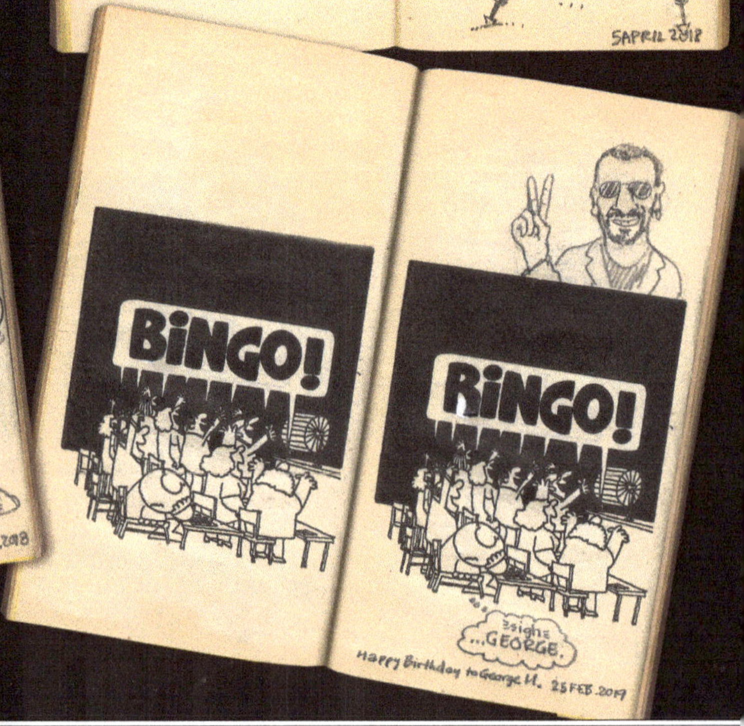
BINGO!
RINGO!
...GEORGE.
Happy Birthday to George H. 25 FEB. 2019

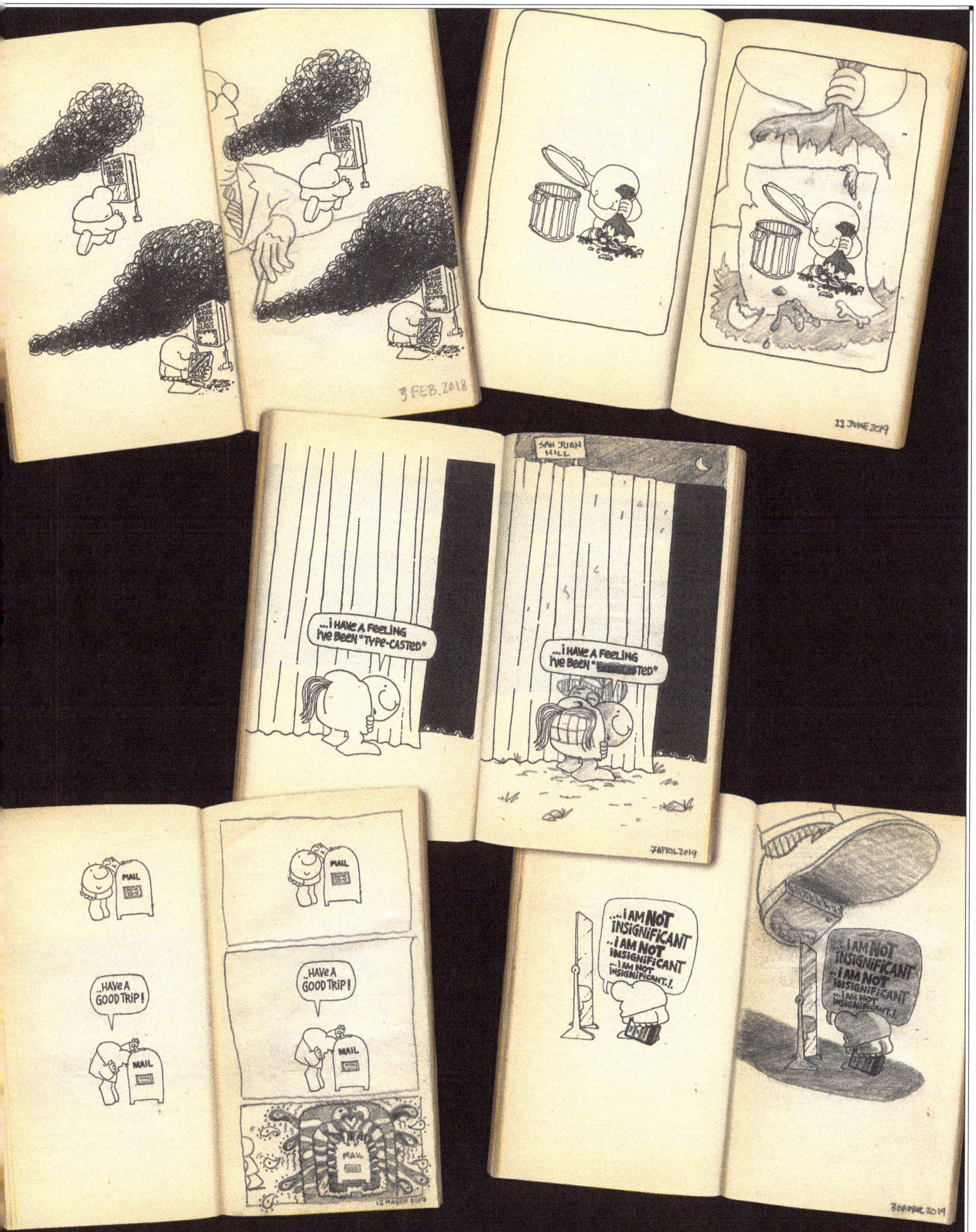
3 FEB. 2018
11 JUNE 2019
...I HAVE A FEELING I'VE BEEN "TYPE-CASTED"
SAN JUAN HILL
7 APRIL 2019
MAIL
..HAVE A GOOD TRIP!
...I AM NOT INSIGNIFICANT
..I AM NOT INSIGNIFICANT
...I AM NOT INSIGNIFICANT.!
30 APRIL 2019

Two-time Eisner Award winning cartoonist & educator
Paul Karasik *can be found on Instagram as karasikkomiks. His non-Z*ggy drawings can be found in* **The New Yorker**. *You can be found reading this.*

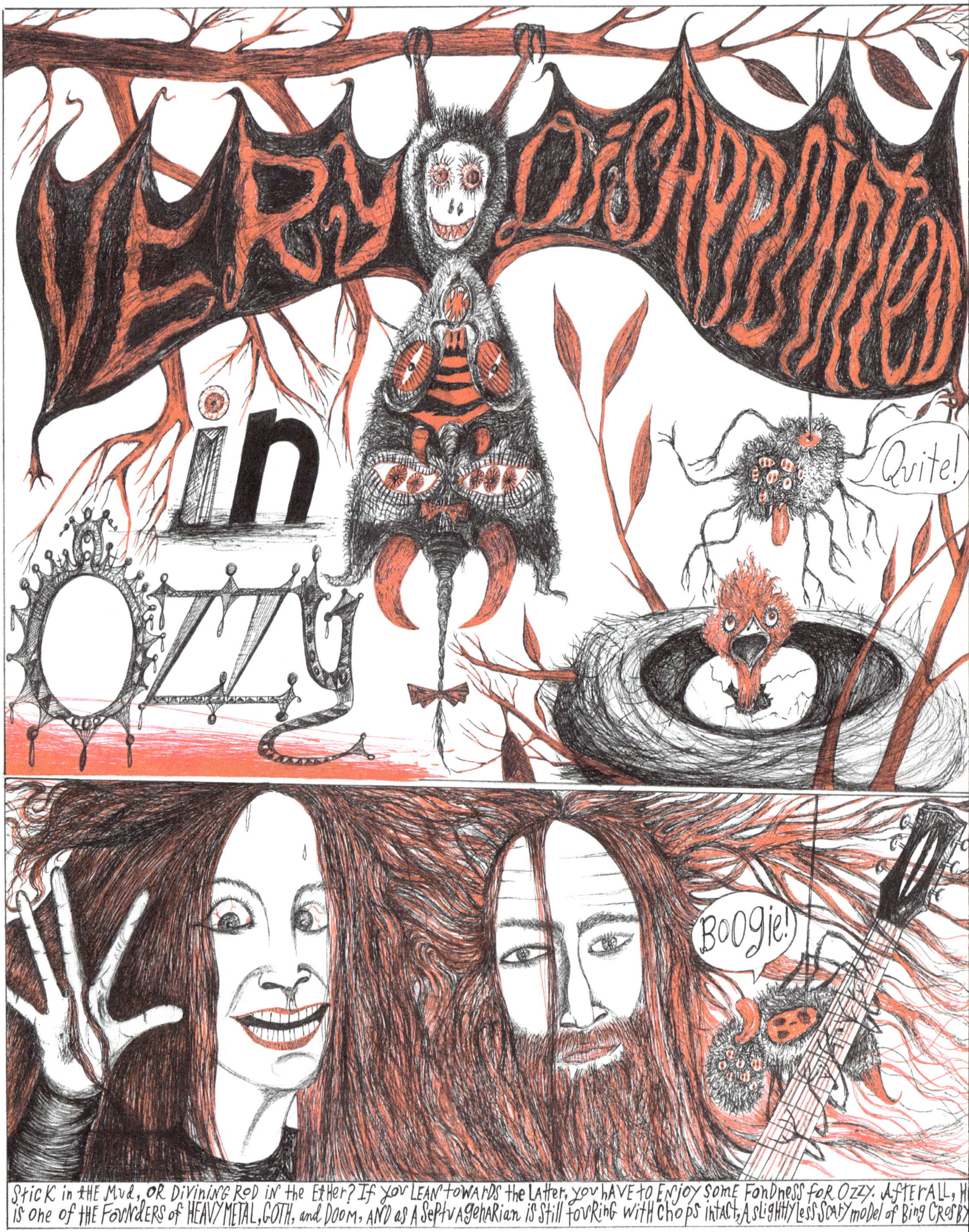
Very Disappointed in Ozzy
Quite!
Boogie!
Stick in the Mud, or Divining Rod in the Ether? If you lean towards the latter, you have to enjoy some fondness for Ozzy. After all, H
is one of the founders of Heavy Metal, Goth, and Doom, and as a septuagenarian is still touring with chops intact, a slightly less scary model of Bing Crosb

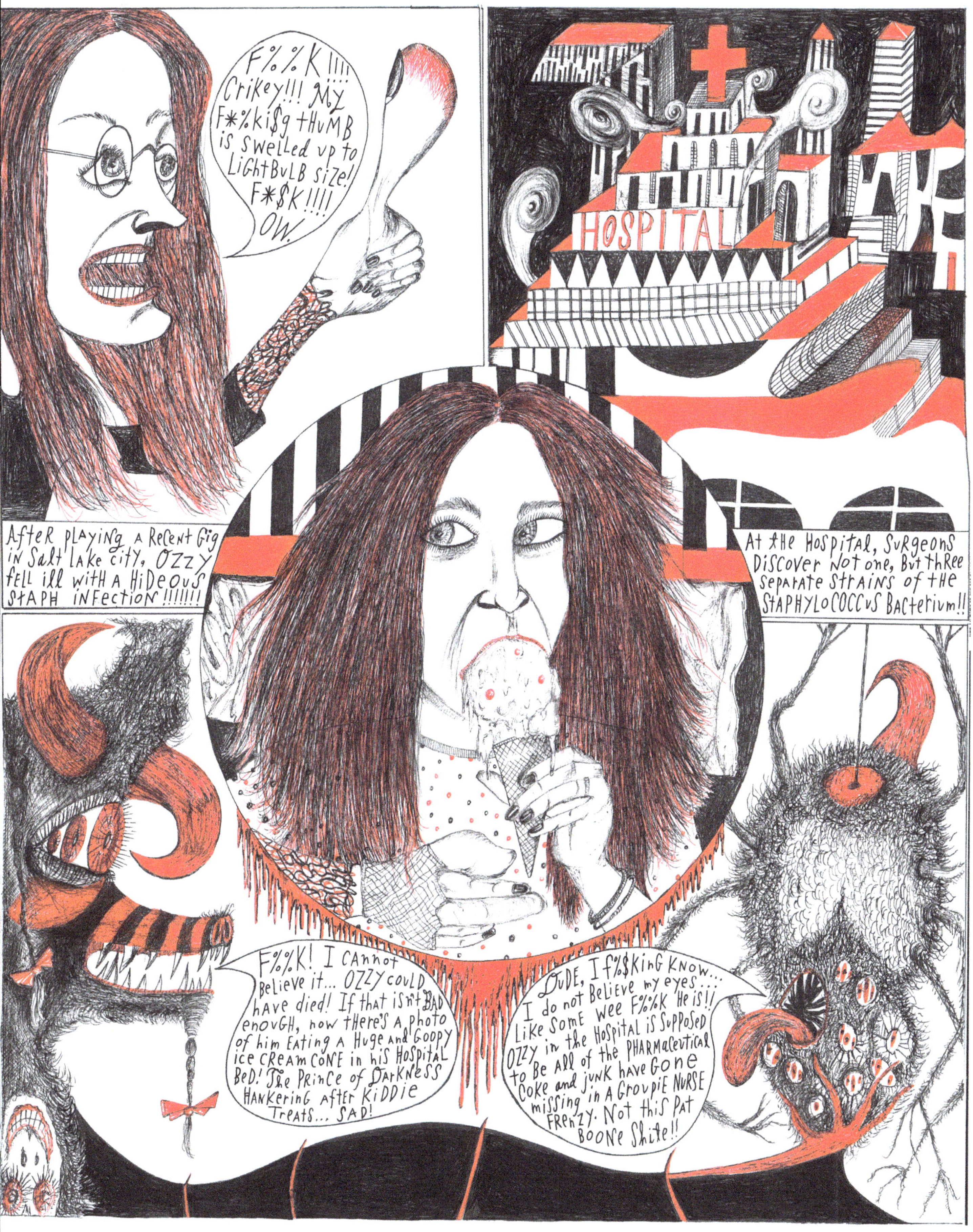

F%%K!!!! Crikey!!! My F*%ki$g tHuMB is Swelled up to LightBuLB size! F*$K!!!! OW.
HOSPITAL
After playing a Recent Gig in Salt Lake city, OZZY fell ill with a Hideous staph infection!!!!!!!
At the Hospital, Surgeons Discover not one, But three separate Strains of the StaPHYLOCOCCUS Bacterium!!
F%%K! I cannot Believe it... OZZY could have died! If that isn't BAD enough, now there's a photo of him Eating a Huge and Goopy ice cream cone in his Hospital Bed! The Prince of Darkness Hankering after Kiddie Treats... SAD!
Dude, I f%$king know... I do not Believe my eyes... Like some wee F%%K He is!! OZZY in the Hospital is supposed to Be All of the pharmaceutical Coke and junk have Gone missing in a Groupie Nurse Frenzy. Not this Pat Boone Shite!!

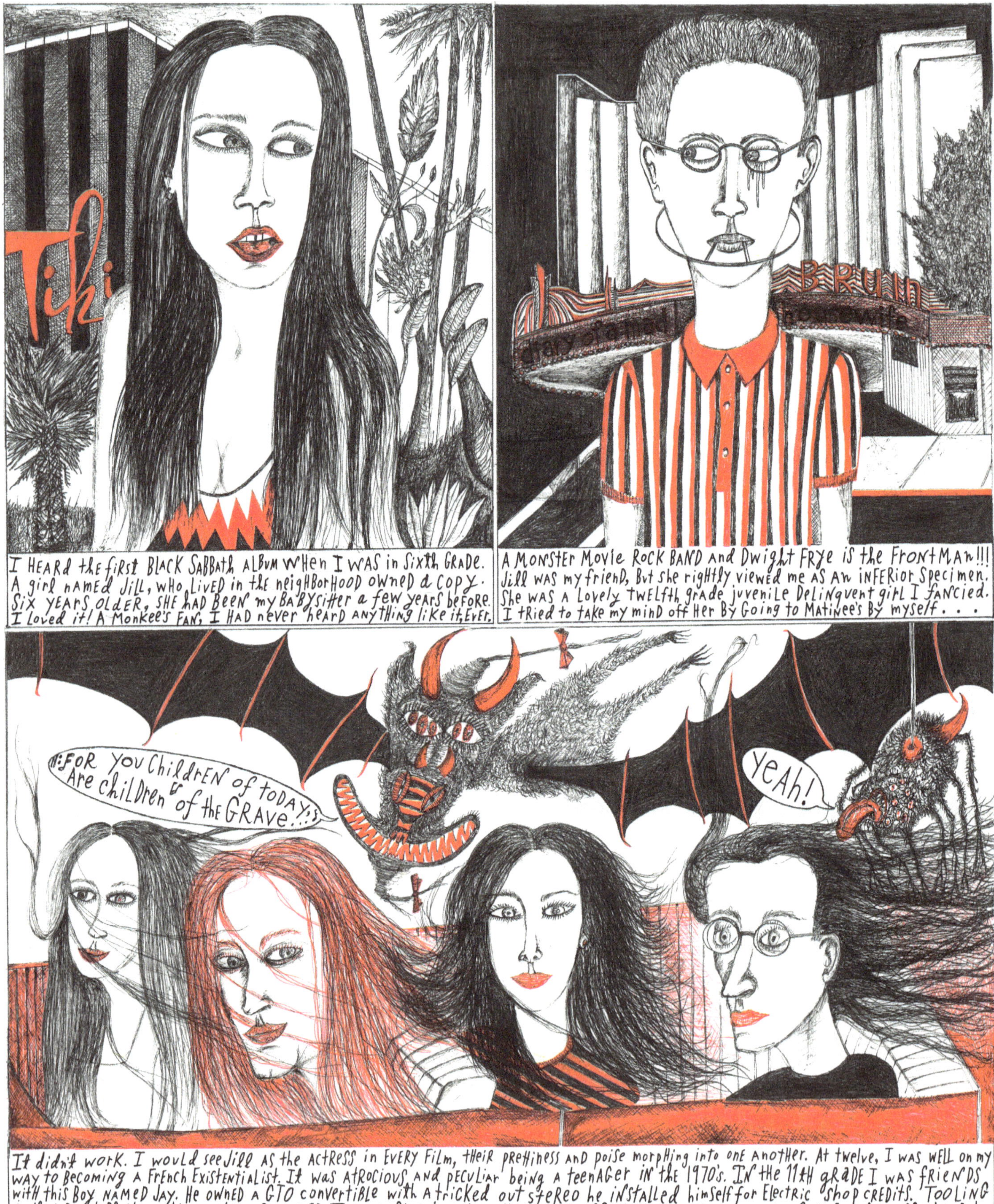
Tiki
diary of a mad
housewife
Bruin
I HEARD the first BLACK SABBATH ALBUM WHEN I WAS in Sixth GRADE. A girl NAMED JILL, WHO LIVED in the neighBorHOOD OWNED a COPY. Six YEARS OLDER, SHE HAD BEEN my BABYSITTER a few years before. I Loved it! A Monkee's FAN, I HAD never heard ANYTHING like it, Ever.
A MONSTER Movie ROCK BAND And Dwight FRye is the FrontMAN!!! Jill WAS my friend, But she rightly viewed me AS AN INFERIOR Specimen. She WAS A Lovely TWELFTH grade juvenile Delinquent girl I fancied. I tried to take my mind off Her By Going to Matinee's By myself. . .
For you Children of today Are children of the GRAVE...
YEAH!
It didn't work. I would see Jill AS the ACTRESS in EVERY Film, their prettiness AND poise morphing into one Another. At twelve, I WAS WELL on my way to Becoming A French Existentialist. It WAS ATROCIOUS AND PECULIAR being A teenAGer in the 1970's. In the 11th gRADE I WAS friends with this Boy NAMED JAY. He OWNED A GTO convertible with A tricked out stereo he installed himself for Electric shop CREDITS. TOOLING in that Beast Blasting the nuclear RAVAGED, Tyrannosaur in A tar pit SOUNDS of SABBATH. At 17 I WAS reading CAMUS And it occurred to me that OZZY WAS Singing ABOUT THE SAME IDEAS THAT CAMUS wrote ABOUT. Likely I WAS WRECKED when I thought this. What would OZZY And Albert Think?

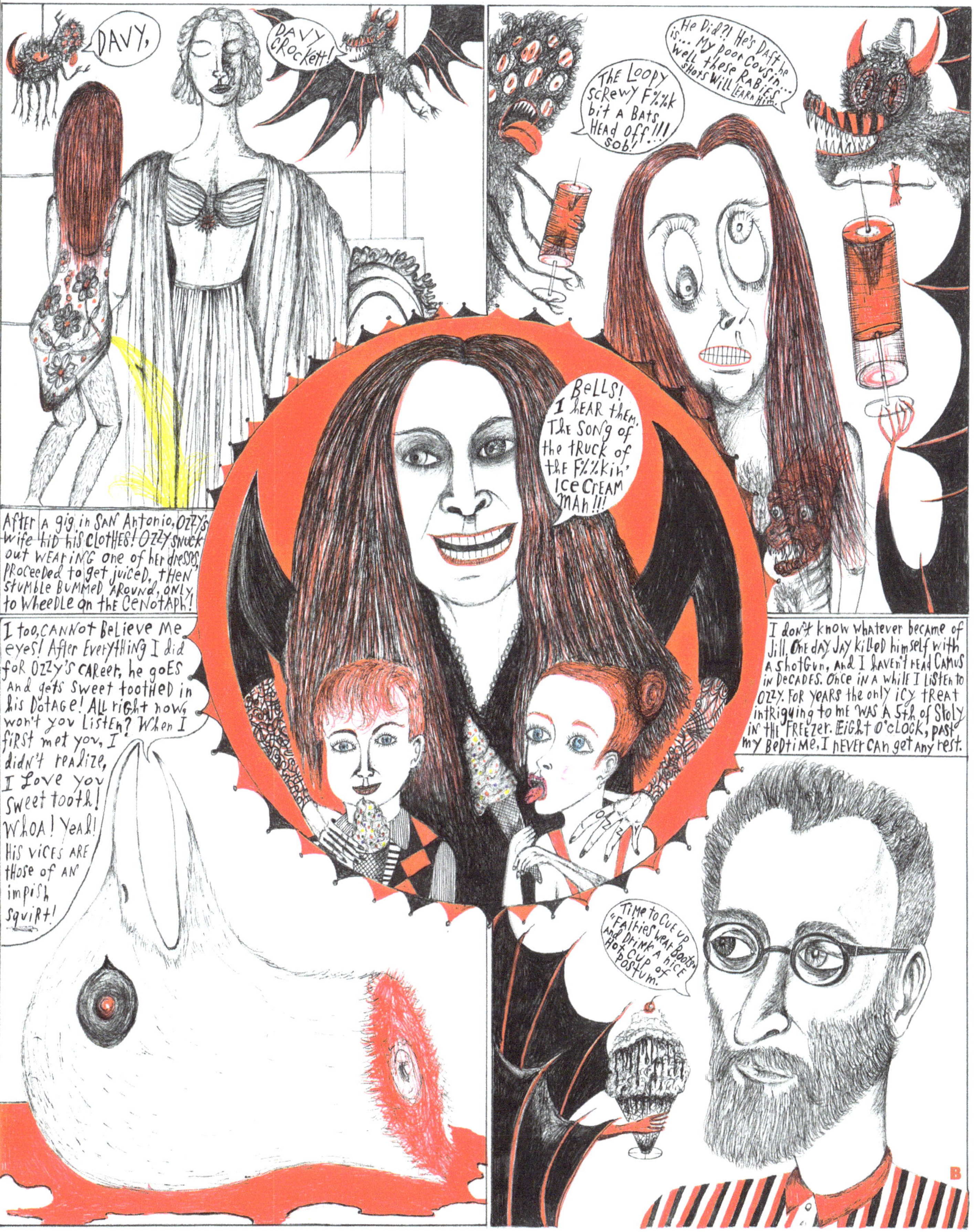
DAVY,
DAVY CROCKett!
THE LOOPY SCREWY F%%k bit A BATS HEAD Off!!! sob!
He Did?! He's DAft he is... My poor Cousin... well these RABIES SHOTS WILL LEARN HIM.
BELLS! I HEAR tHEM. THE SONG OF the tRUCK of the F%%kin' ICE CREAM MAN!!!
After a gig in SAN Antonio, OZZY's wife hid his CLOTHES! OZZY snuck out WEARING one of her dresses, PROCEEDED to get juiced, tHEN stumble BUMMED AROUND, ONLY to WHEEDLE on the CENOTAPH!
I don't know whatever became of Jill. One day Jay killed himself with a shotGun, And I haven't read Camus in DECADES. Once in a while I Listen to OZZY. For years the only icy treat intriguing to me was a 5th of Stoly in the FREEZER. Eight O'CLOCK, past my BEDTIME. I never can get any rest.
I too, CANNOT Believe me eyes! After Everything I did for OZZY'S CAREER, he goES And gets sweet toothed in his DOTAGE! ALL right now, won't you Listen? When I first met you, I didn't realize, I Love you sweet tooth! WHOA! Yeah! His VICES ARE those of AN impish squirt!
Time to Cue up "Fairies wear Boots" And Drink A nice Hot CUP of POSTUM.
B

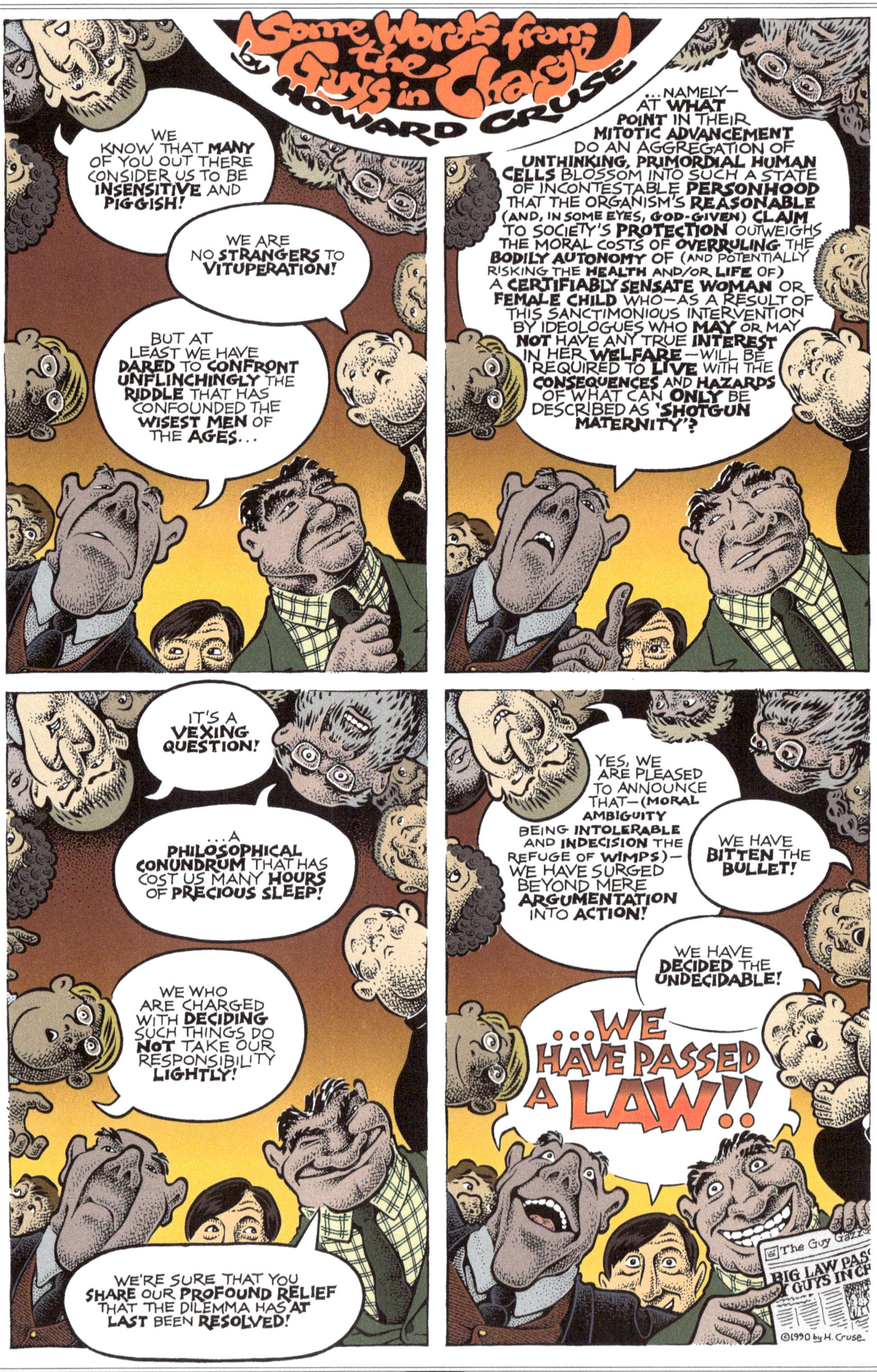

Some Words from the Guys in Charge
by HOWARD CRUSE
WE KNOW THAT MANY OF YOU OUT THERE CONSIDER US TO BE INSENSITIVE AND PIGGISH!
WE ARE NO STRANGERS TO VITUPERATION!
BUT AT LEAST WE HAVE DARED TO CONFRONT UNFLINCHINGLY THE RIDDLE THAT HAS CONFOUNDED THE WISEST MEN OF THE AGES...
...NAMELY—AT WHAT POINT IN THEIR MITOTIC ADVANCEMENT DO AN AGGREGATION OF UNTHINKING, PRIMORDIAL HUMAN CELLS BLOSSOM INTO SUCH A STATE OF INCONTESTABLE PERSONHOOD THAT THE ORGANISM'S REASONABLE (AND, IN SOME EYES, GOD-GIVEN) CLAIM TO SOCIETY'S PROTECTION OUTWEIGHS THE MORAL COSTS OF OVERRULING THE BODILY AUTONOMY OF (AND POTENTIALLY RISKING THE HEALTH AND/OR LIFE OF) A CERTIFIABLY SENSATE WOMAN OR FEMALE CHILD WHO—AS A RESULT OF THIS SANCTIMONIOUS INTERVENTION BY IDEOLOGUES WHO MAY OR MAY NOT HAVE ANY TRUE INTEREST IN HER WELFARE—WILL BE REQUIRED TO LIVE WITH THE CONSEQUENCES AND HAZARDS OF WHAT CAN ONLY BE DESCRIBED AS 'SHOTGUN MATERNITY'?
IT'S A VEXING QUESTION!
...A PHILOSOPHICAL CONUNDRUM THAT HAS COST US MANY HOURS OF PRECIOUS SLEEP!
WE WHO ARE CHARGED WITH DECIDING SUCH THINGS DO NOT TAKE OUR RESPONSIBILITY LIGHTLY!
WE'RE SURE THAT YOU SHARE OUR PROFOUND RELIEF THAT THE DILEMMA HAS AT LAST BEEN RESOLVED!
YES, WE ARE PLEASED TO ANNOUNCE THAT—(MORAL AMBIGUITY BEING INTOLERABLE AND INDECISION THE REFUGE OF WIMPS)—WE HAVE SURGED BEYOND MERE ARGUMENTATION INTO ACTION!
WE HAVE BITTEN THE BULLET!
WE HAVE DECIDED THE UNDECIDABLE!
...WE HAVE PASSED A LAW!!
©1990 by H. Cruse

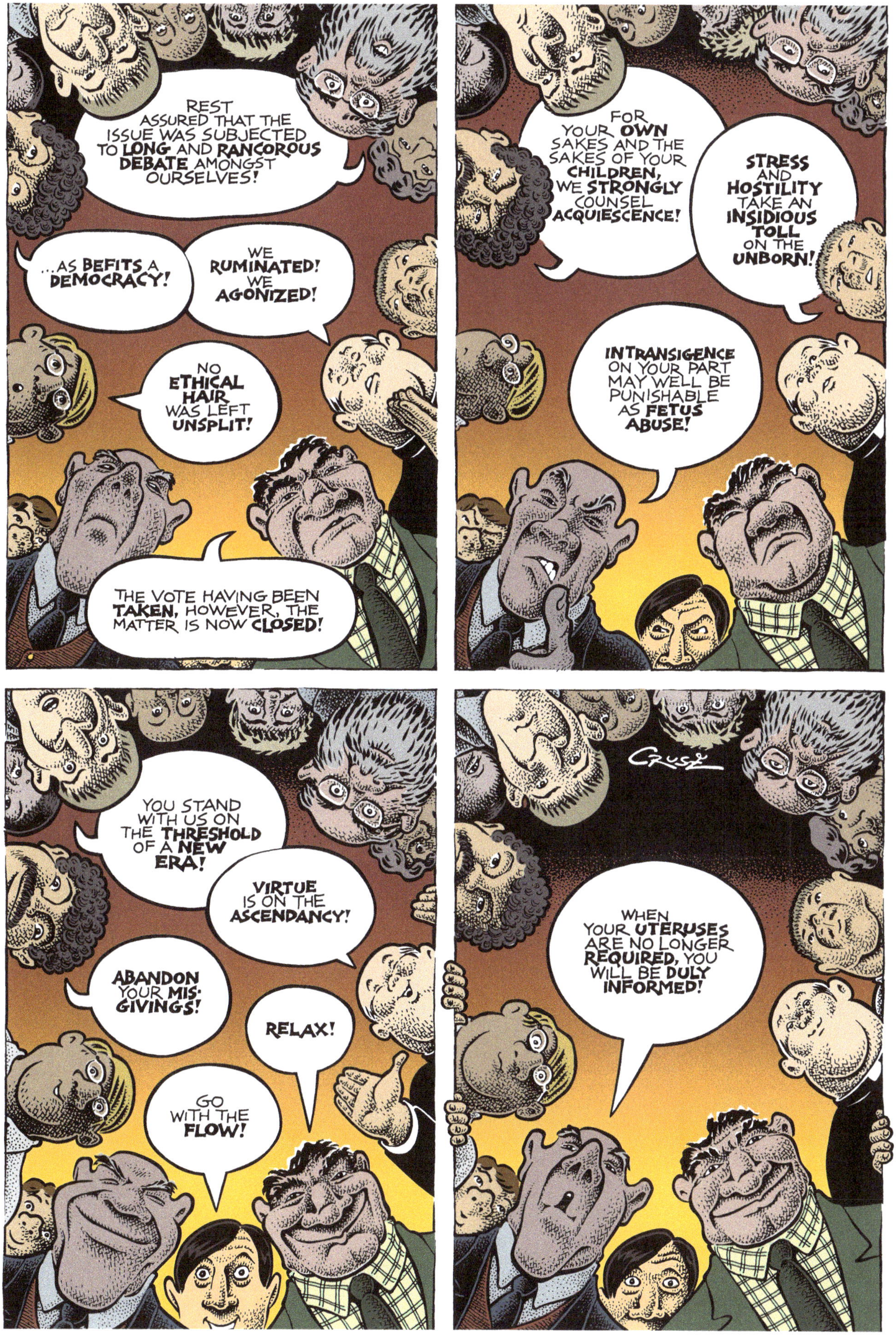
REST ASSURED THAT THE ISSUE WAS SUBJECTED TO LONG AND RANCOROUS DEBATE AMONGST OURSELVES!
...AS BEFITS A DEMOCRACY!
WE RUMINATED! WE AGONIZED!
NO ETHICAL HAIR WAS LEFT UNSPLIT!
THE VOTE HAVING BEEN TAKEN, HOWEVER, THE MATTER IS NOW CLOSED!
FOR YOUR OWN SAKES AND THE SAKES OF YOUR CHILDREN, WE STRONGLY COUNSEL ACQUIESCENCE!
STRESS AND HOSTILITY TAKE AN INSIDIOUS TOLL ON THE UNBORN!
INTRANSIGENCE ON YOUR PART MAY WELL BE PUNISHABLE AS FETUS ABUSE!
YOU STAND WITH US ON THE THRESHOLD OF A NEW ERA!
VIRTUE IS ON THE ASCENDANCY!
ABANDON YOUR MIS-GIVINGS!
RELAX!
GO WITH THE FLOW!
CRUSE
WHEN YOUR UTERUSES ARE NO LONGER REQUIRED, YOU WILL BE DULY INFORMED!

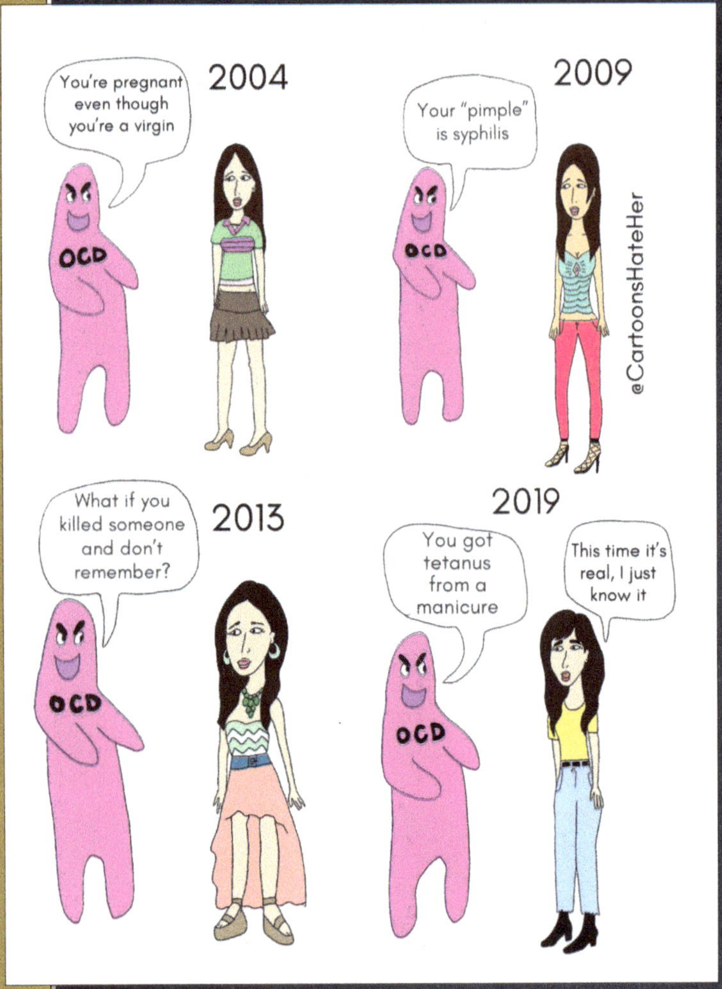
2004
You're pregnant even though you're a virgin
OCD
2009
Your "pimple" is syphilis
OCD
@CartoonsHateHer
2013
What if you killed someone and don't remember?
OCD
2019
You got tetanus from a manicure
OCD
This time it's real, I just know it

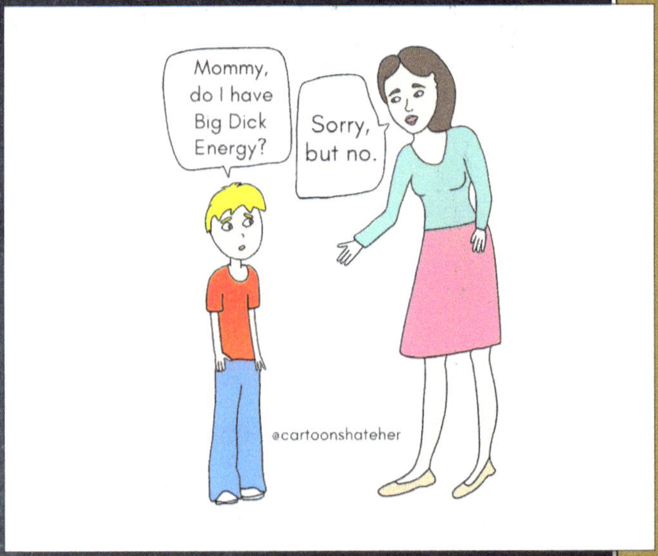
Mommy, do I have Big Dick Energy?
Sorry, but no.
@cartoonshateher

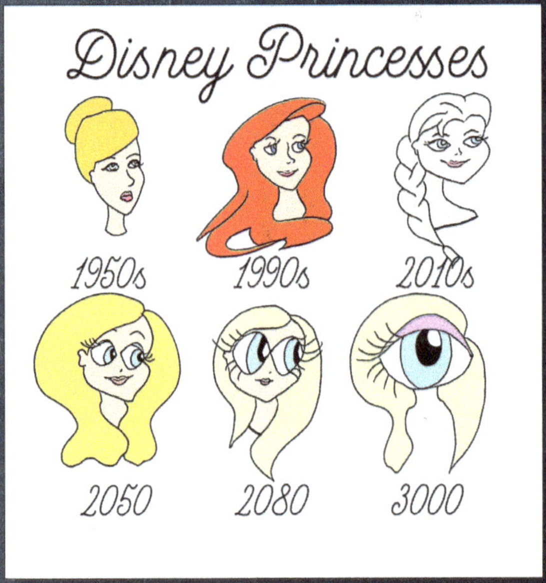
Disney Princesses
1950s
1990s
2010s
2050
2080
3000

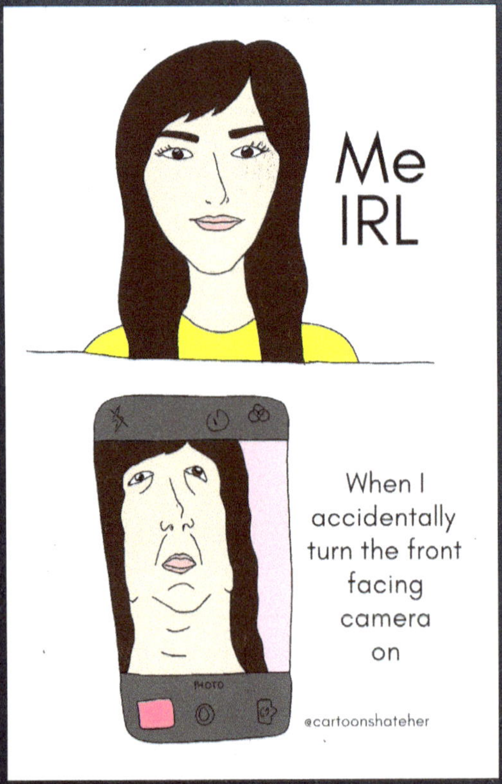
Me IRL
When I accidentally turn the front facing camera on
PHOTO
@cartoonshateher

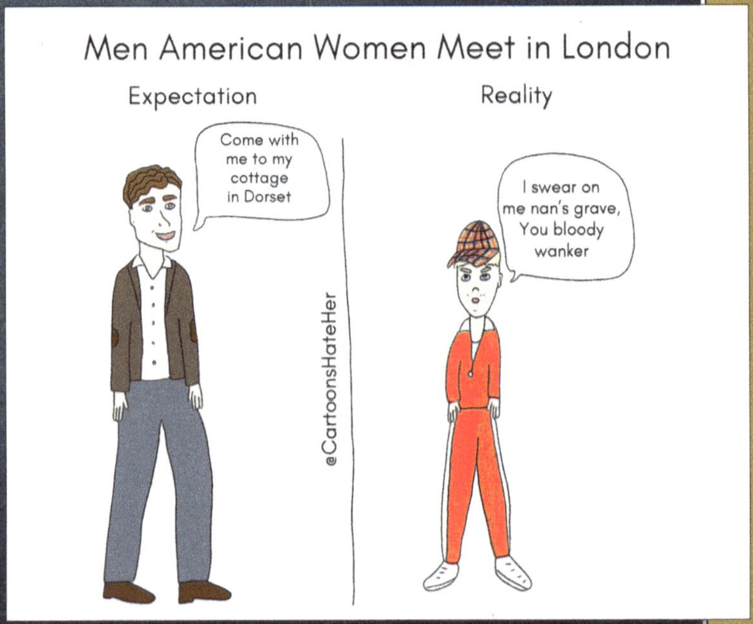
Men American Women Meet in London
Expectation
Reality
Come with me to my cottage in Dorset
I swear on me nan's grave, You bloody wanker
@CartoonsHateHer

The Funniest Two Books
Since the Old and New Testament

Princeton Architectural Press

www.papress.com

THESE COLORS WILL MAKE YOU FEEL HUNGRY
FIND A UNIQUE RESTAURANT EXPERIENCE
IN JOHN DONOHUE'S NEW BOOK

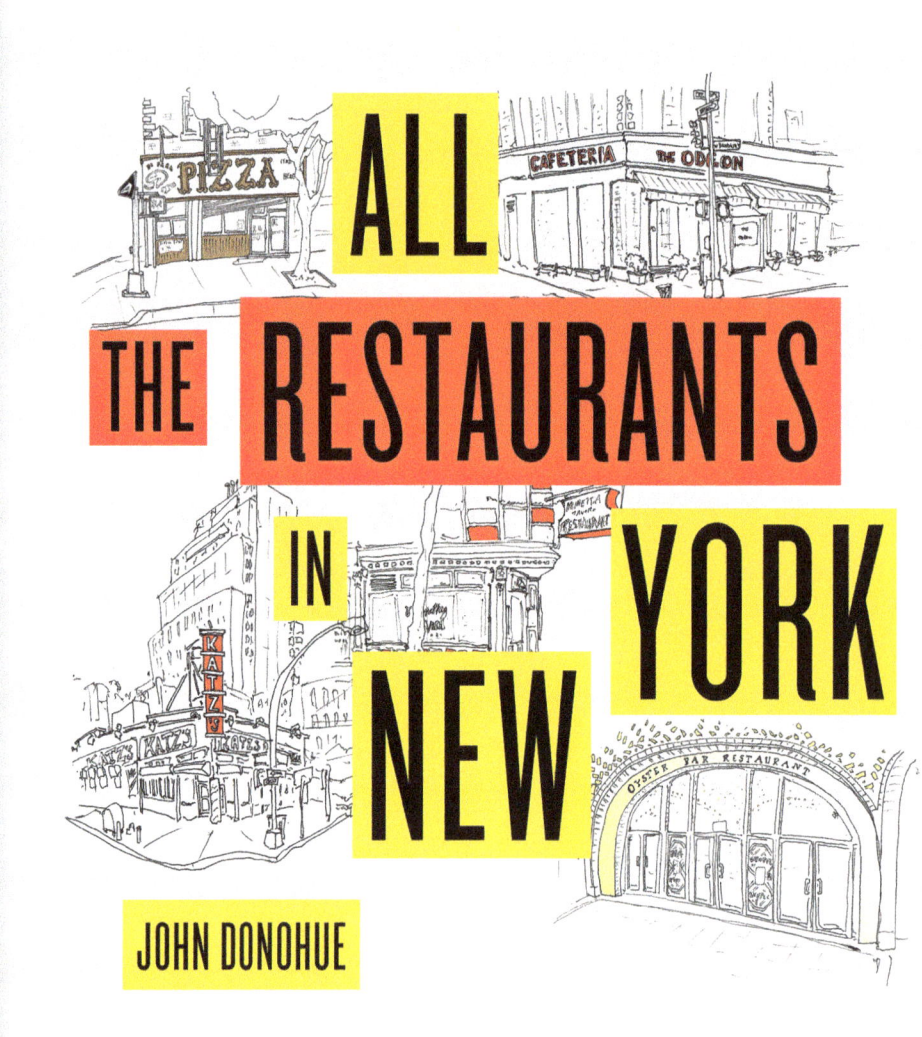

"John Donohue is the Rembrandt of New York City's restaurant facades."
—**Adam Platt**, restaurant critic, *New York* magazine

"If you know someone who's wild for a special New York restaurant, this is the perfect present."
-**Ruth Reichl**

Includes *that* Italian restaurant that brings in grandmothers from around the world to cook!

Available in fine bookstores everywhere
Find signed, limited-edition prints at alltherestaurants.com

OUR BACK PAGES

LETTER FROM MELANIA

FLOTUS goes through "the change," and numberless dimensions tremble • By Emily Flake

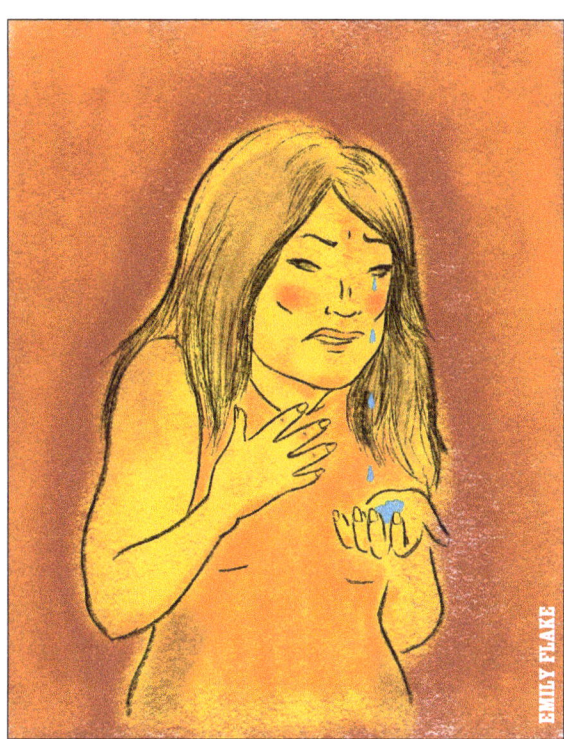

BORUTA! I invoke thee! BCHORT! I invoke thee! DREKAVAC, LECHIES and RUSALKA, I invoke thee! My fellow demons, I know you must be wondering why I have summoned you to this group chat. As you are all well aware, the Plan is succeeding beyond any of our wildest dreams (except perhaps yours, Rusalka, you've always been such an optimist!). The mortals are at each other's throats, day and night, even while on the toilet. The surface of this dying world continues to deteriorate at a pace matched only by the swift crumbling of Donald's fragile psyche. I could not be better pleased, and I am sure you feel the same.

However, it is with concerns about deterioration of another sort that I come to you with today. The human form you have given me has performed its objective remarkably well, and I will say without bragging that I have more than upheld my end of the bargain, denying it any kind of sensual pleasure, punishing it with endless Pilates, and using it to give earthly form to the one we call B****n, when we must say his Name at all. My body is a machine, kept well-oiled by the blood of frequent sacrifice (and more than a little Crème de la Mer).

However, even a machine as perfectly maintained as my own cannot last forever. This is becoming abundantly clear to me as the connection of this body to its monthly rhythms begins to fray. My moon-times have become erratic, which make my physical duties to Donald difficult to schedule, given his childish terror when faced with female blood. I myself do not relish these activities, but I find that after them, he is even more pliant and suggestible than usual. Some of my best work is done in this afterglow, but how am I supposed to lure Donald to the marital bed if I am constantly dripping feminine ichor?

Many times, I have been interrupted in my tasks by a sudden, full-body sensation of heat. I cannot express to you how disappointing it is when I realize that the sensation comes not from the glorious chthonic fire come to consume this world at last, but from my own suddenly unpredictable flesh. Are you familiar with the human emotion known as "embarrassment?" I cannot recommend it.

Other human emotions begin, alarmingly, to take root in the cracks of this failing vessel. My eyes have begun to leak, often at inopportune moments. Just yesterday I saw a video about a lost dog and had to hide in a closet until the leaking stopped. I have found it necessary to lie down in the middle of the day and stare at the ceiling for hours on end. I crave, to my utter dismay, sugar mixed with fat. Oh hell and damnation, there go my eye-holes again.

And friends—one of the three decorative hairs I keep on my *mons pubis* has turned white.

If this form cannot be salvaged, I am prepared to let it go. I do not mean to let it die—despite the fact that my milk dried up long ago, B****n has made it clear he is still not ready to be weaned—but I do suggest we reinstate the soul that originally dwelled in this body (Drekavic, if you've eaten it, I'm going to be very cross). It is sure to be a bit worse for wear after its long exile to the Shadowlands, but it need only be able to smile, wave, and answer soft-ball questions from sympathetic journalists. As for me, I think it best that I take up residence in one of the children. Either Don Jr. or Ivanka will do (though I am not looking forward to the continuation of my physical duties to Donald, if we go that route). Eric is obviously a non-starter, as it would raise too many suspicions if he suddenly began to speak in complete sentences. I would prefer to keep Tiffany for spare parts.

I propose that we begin preparations for the Ritual as soon as demonically possible. I simply cannot bear another minute spent wondering if the skin on my neck can take another tightening procedure (*NB*: it cannot). I thank you for the sacrifice of your time.

It Won't Be Long Now,
Melania

EMILY FLAKE is FLOTUS Whisperer for *The American Bystander*.

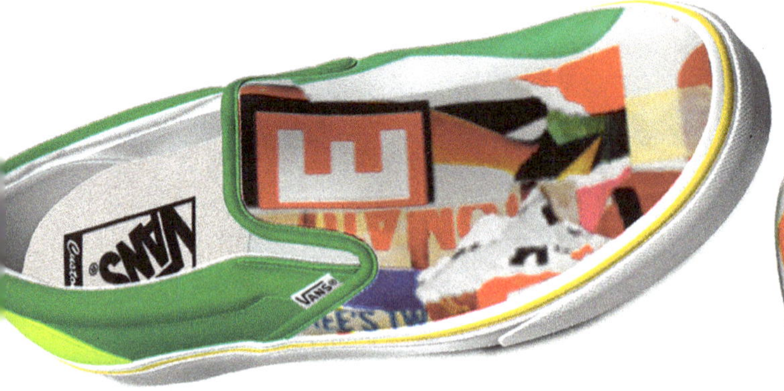

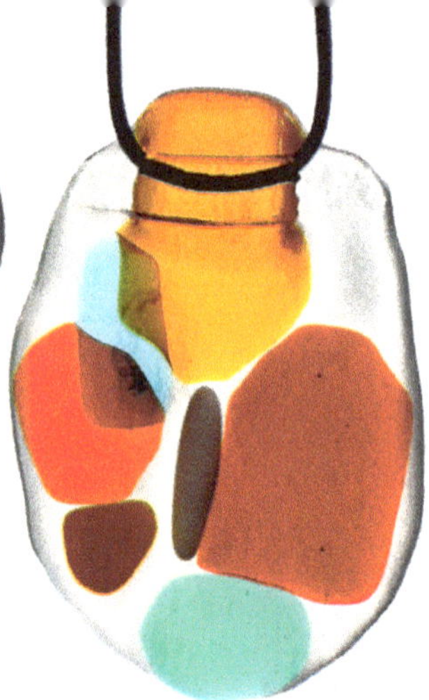

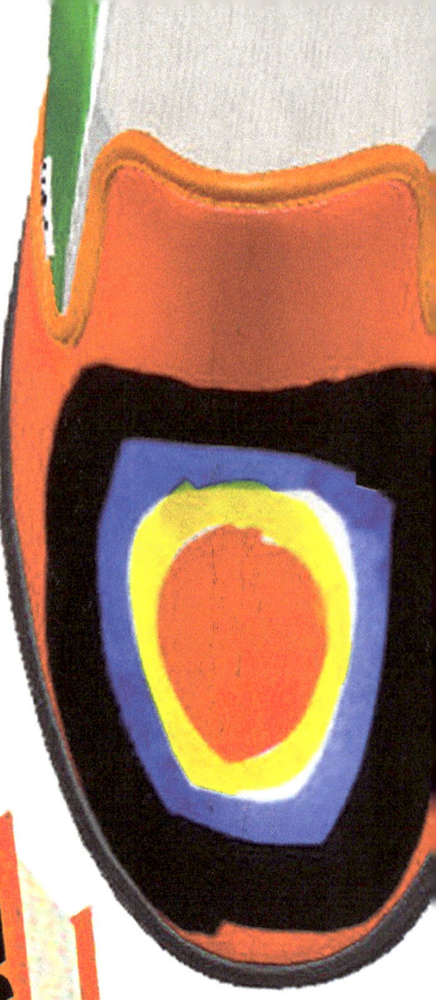

visit www.rosenworld.com

for
Sneakers, Signed Books,
Melty Jewels
and Original Artwork
by Laurie Rosenwald, First Pancake,
Occasional Swede

& America's Favorite Bystander

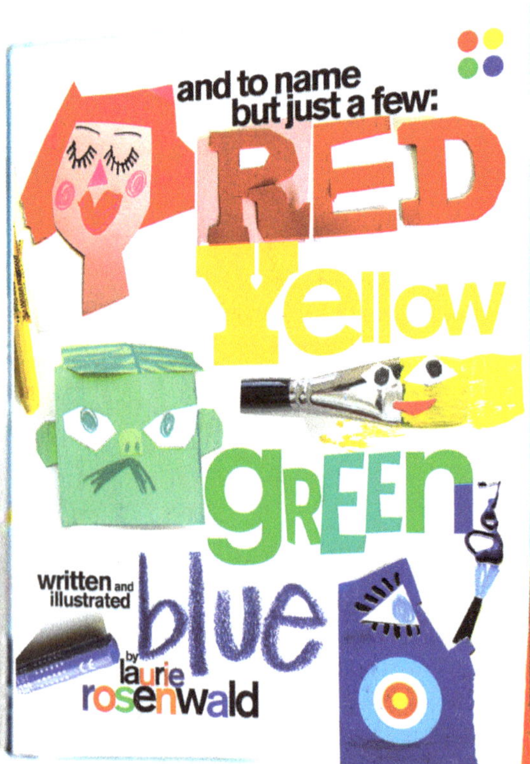
and to name but just a few:
RED
Yellow
GREEN
blue
written and illustrated by laurie rosenwald

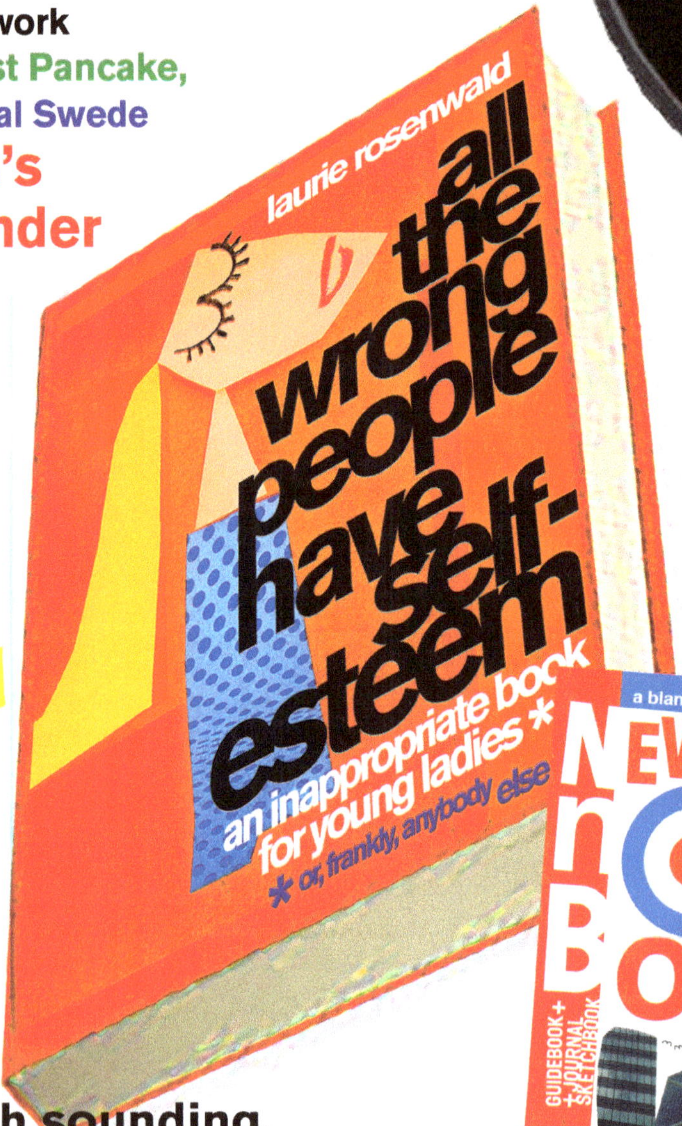
laurie rosenwald
all the wrong people have self-esteem
an inappropriate book for young ladies *
* or, frankly, anybody else

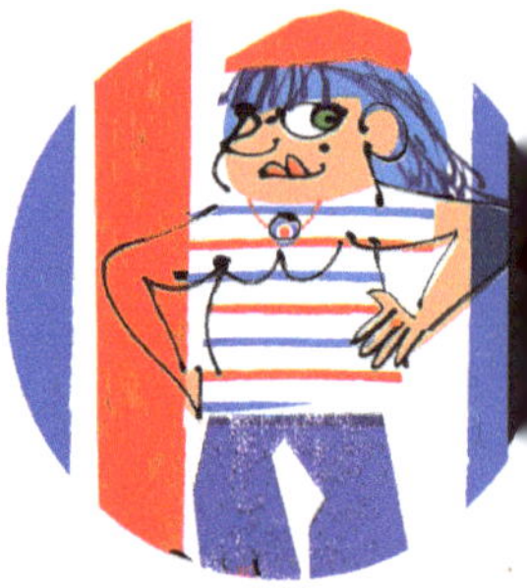

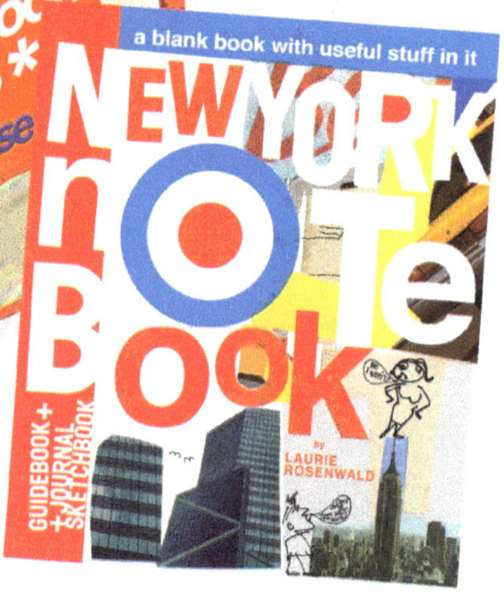
a blank book with useful stuff in it
NEW YORK NOTE BOOK
GUIDEBOOK + JOURNAL + SKETCHBOOK
by LAURIE ROSENWALD

"Laurie's voice is fresh sounding, funny, and completely her own." -David Sedaris

OUR BACK PAGES

WHAT AM I DOING HERE?

Walking against the wind, in the Land of the Ritz Auschwitz • By Mike Reiss

Slaughterhouse Five-Star Hotel

If there were a Museum of Bad Ideas, the main exhibit would be… well, the museum itself. It's a terrible concept. But the second-worst idea might be this: "Let's turn an old industrial slaughterhouse into a luxury hotel!"

The problem is not that someone tried this—it's that they didn't try hard enough. From the outside, this posh resort in southern Chile looks like a death camp, because that's what it was: a century ago, up to 250,000 sheep were butchered here—each year! To access the hotel's Zen spa, you have to walk through the same concrete chute thousands of lambs were funneled through on their trip to the stockyards. To get to their elegant dining room, you have to pass through the Gallery of Carnage: a cavernous, drafty hall decorated with sepia photos of lambs being skinned and hung on hooks. *Bon appetit!*

If I were a vegan, this place would be the Ritz Auschwitz. But even though I love eating little lambs, it still creeped me out. My room was cozy and beautifully appointed, but when I lay down in bed, I could see they'd kept the old abattoir ceiling: rusty steel plates with a single bare bulb sticking out. The decor was an uncomfortable mix of *Downton Abbey* and *Saw*.

MIKE REISS is Intrepid Traveler for *The American Bystander*.

On Christmas Day, my beautiful wife climbed the world's ugliest mountains.

Another problem with this hotel—and it really didn't need another problem—was that every single employee in every single department was bad at their job: reception, housekeeping, and especially the bar staff. Every night I'd order "*una cerveza*" just to see what they'd bring: a whiskey sour, a bowl of peanuts, nothing, a cup of coffee, the hotel manager—anything but a beer. Ordering became a Dada exercise.

There were sheep who had a better time here than me.

Of course, it's hard to find good help when you build your hotel in one of the least-populated spots on the planet: Patagonia. But with its snow-capped mountains, crystal-blue rivers, and sweeping golden plains, there's no place quite like Patagonia. Except Montana. And Colorado. And Utah. And Idaho, I imagine. But Patagonia has one thing all those places don't have: persistent gale-force winds.

In Patagonia, ahe wind blows all the freaking time, and like Patagonia itself, it blows hard.*

The travel agent who sent us here neglected to mention this. But everyone else couldn't stop talking about it:

TOUR GUIDE: *This was the last place on Earth man settled in, due to the high winds…*
FJORD CRUISE CAPTAIN: *There are at least three reasons for Patagonia's high winds…*
HOTEL CLERK: *You might wear these earplugs to bed to block the noise of the high winds…*

It's windy because there's no other land at this latitude. Even Pangaea knew not to come here. If you don't believe me, look at a map. (You're not gonna look at a map.) All the wind in the lower Southern Hemisphere hits Patagonia, because there is nothing else on Earth to stop it. It's a great place to visit, if you're a kite.

When I called the travel agent to complain, she said, "Patagonia is lovely, except for the wind." Which is like saying, "Lung cancer is a lot of fun, except for the cancer." (In fact, the tobacco companies have said just that.) So why do people travel here? It's the name: Patagonia. It sounds so romantic one friend asked me, "You mean that's a real place?" Of course, the name loses a little in translation. It's like the Bolshoi Ballet: it sounds so classy, but bolshoi just means big. Bolshoi Ballet? Big Ballet. Big deal.

According to legend, when Magellan first visited Patagonia, he saw an Indian's

---

*To be honest, the wind stops blowing during the winter, when Patagonia is too cold to visit. But when summer comes and the suckers return, the warm air rises creating a vacuum, which is filled by cold gusting winds from nearby Antarctica. This has inspired my new comedy series *It's Always Sucky in Patagonia*.

OWN ORIGINAL CARTOON ART

Become the owner—or gift giver— of original artwork.

Sam Gross

"IT SORT OF MAKES YOU STOP AND THINK, DOESN'T IT."

P.C. Vey

George Booth

To enquire about your favorites please contact Samantha Vuignier:

SamanthaVuignier@CartoonCollections.com

or visit

CartoonCollections.com/originals

CARTOON COLLECTIONS

CARTOONCOLLECTIONS.COM

---

huge footprint in the snow—the natives stood almost a foot taller than the European invaders. "These people have feet like ducks (*patos*)," Magellan is said to have remarked. "Let's kill them all."

"Patagonia" is a terrific name for a sportswear company. "Land of People with Duck Feet"? Not so much.

Patagonia has lovely glaciers you can cruise by, but to reach the tour boat, you have to walk across a mile-wide valley where the winds gust at eighty MPH. Storm-chasers avoid weather like this. The gales literally blew my mouth open and began inflating me like a party balloon. When I finally reached the boat, the captain told me, "The water's a little rough today, but don't worry, we have a Plan B." A few minutes later, the trip was canceled due to (brace yourself) high winds.

"So what's Plan B?" I asked.

"We have no Plan B," he replied.

That is Patagonia.

There is, in fact, just one other tourist attraction here. It's called *Tres Torres*— three giant black squares of rock jutting out of a mountain top. To me, they looked like something out of Dante: Satan's rotting teeth.

It's a four-hour, near-vertical climb to reach the Devil's Dentures, with the wind pushing you back at each step. Everything about this place said, "Don't go there." My wife wanted to go there.

A good husband would never send his wife on this life-threatening hike alone, so clearly I suck. Denise and I have been together for thirty years; we could spend one random day apart. This random day happened to be December 25th.

So my wife spent Christmas making this grueling climb, while I remained in the comfort at the Abattoir Suites Hotel. That's where I wrote this story, while enjoying an ice-cold *cerveza*.

Of course, what I'd ordered was a club sandwich.

OUR BACK PAGES

P.S. MUELLER THINKS LIKE THIS
The cartoonist/broadcaster/writer is always walking around, looking at stuff • By P.S. Mueller

"Look, we're live-streaming!"

Mascots Must Feed

Beginning in the last century, the world's mascot population abruptly grew with Malthusian intensity and they are everywhere today. Everywhere except farms. You will find them waving from the side of the road, dancing in front of hardware stores, working the periphery of funerals—everywhere. But what do we know about them, really? Not much, I'm afraid. They expend energy, and so, they must consume calories in order to maintain constant high levels of enthusiasm for: openings, closings, sporting events. Yes, mascots must feed.

There are two types of mascot. The human mascot is just a guy inhabiting some kind of comical foam-rubber shell. Their mouths are Muppet-like and they are all distinguished by what we here at the Reaseach Bureau call "the Henson crease." These mascots are harmless and pose no threat of any kind. They survive mainly on hot dogs.

The other type of mascot is not human. Upon examination, their mouths contain a large hole descending to their midsection, apparently going nowhere beyond that. They digest all of what they eat and never need to use the facilities. We here at the Research Bureau, after decades of study, now believe that these inhuman mascots consume small people.

One of our numbers people happened to notice a correlation between the decline of horse racing and the rise of mascots are few years ago, which led to a grisly discovery that jockeys had been going missing in ever-greater numbers. Indeed, horse racing events appeared to attract mascots. Jockey survivors were aware of the phenomenon but kept it to themselves, not wanting to be labeled "crazy and small." It may be that jockeys are all crazy and small, but we won't know until our people in the field return with tiny photographs and bits of data. Still, the clues are all there.

Today horse racing is nearly gone, yet larger numbers of small people continue to disappear. Petite models, oil change pit-workers, and such. Actor Tom Cruise now seems to be fair game for these unspeakably ravenous foam rubber homunculi. Cruise no longer appears in public unless surrounded by a half dozen Vin Diesel body doubles. And even then, Cruise has gotten quite jumpy. (However, some witnesses maintain that Cruise has always been jumpy, and we're working on that as well.)

These deadly mascots, we now know, are most vulnerable on their "mating day"—which happens to be on Halloween. In order to procreate, one mascot must literally crawl into its partner. (Gender doesn't apply to any of this.) This can be very painful for the entrant, resulting in what we here at the Research Bureau call "the muffled shriek." Foam-rubber can also tear during mating, which may explain all those horrible sounds coming from nearby hills this time of year.

Several hours after mating, two fully formed mascots emerge by way of some kind of budding process, and they are hungry for Size 6 humans. Oddly, they have no taste for children as it is believed that kids leave an aftertaste repugnant to the monsters. Farmers know this and make a point of producing many children. Farmers have also kept this information to themselves because, deep down, farmers just want the rest of us to crawl off and die of rickets or something. This is a farmer thing that the Research Bureau isn't about to study or investigate.

Can these bouncy smiling and waving mascot creatures be killed? *Yes.* We're working on that. B

P.S. MUELLER is Staff Liar of *The American Bystander*.

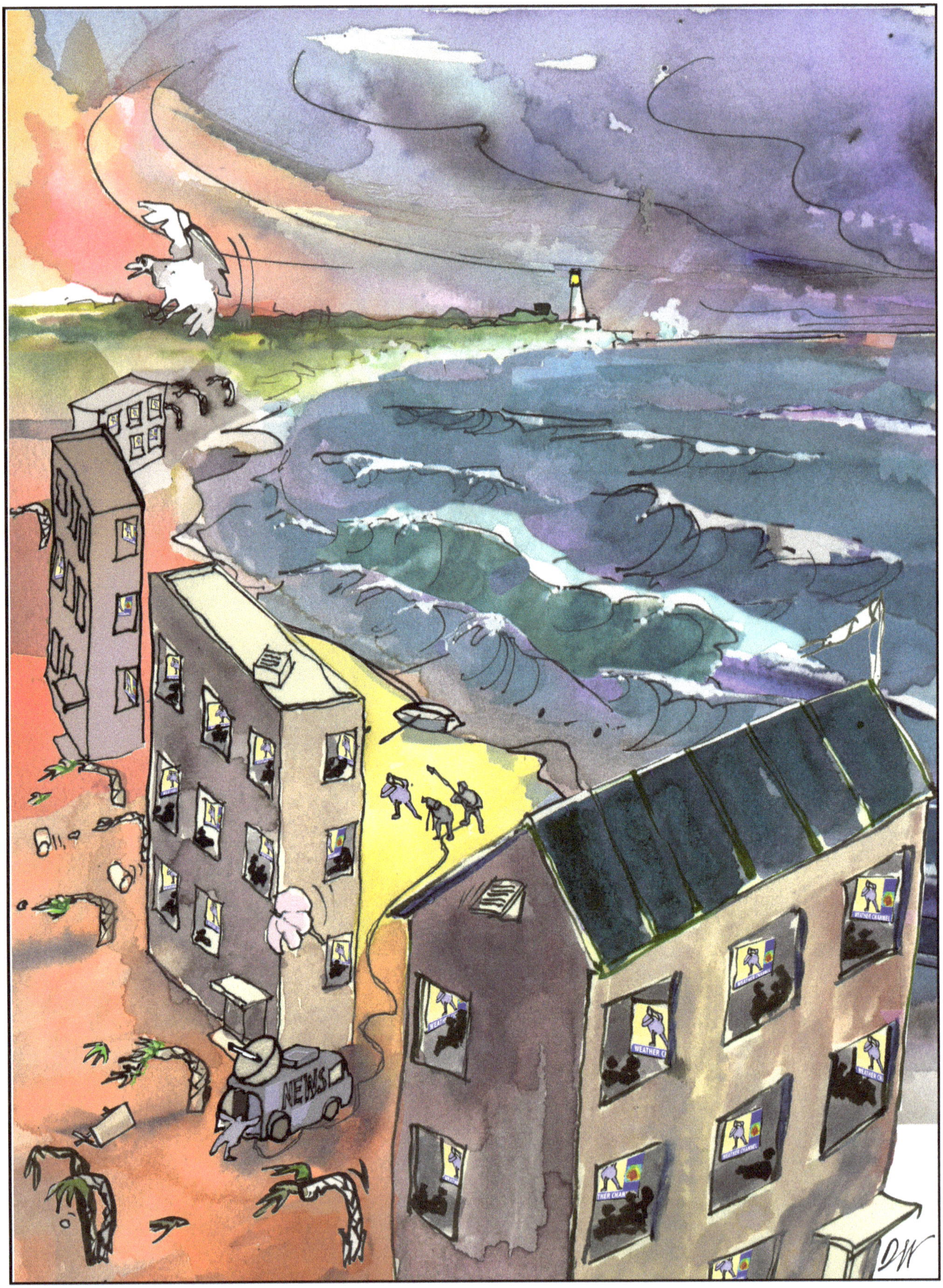
NEWS
WEATHER CHANNEL

D. WATSON *is the pen name of D. Watson, released on his own recognizance from various institutions, living in Connecticut in a witless protection program.*

www.ingramcontent.com/pod-product-compliance
Lightning Source LLC
Chambersburg PA
CBHW061755290426
44108CB00029B/2999